Engineering Foundations: The Pillars of Modern Software Craftsmanship

Engineering Foundations: The Pillars of Modern Software Craftsmanship

Timeless Principles and Modern Practices for Building Systems That Last

Dmytro Golodiuk

2025

Engineering Foundations: The Pillars of Modern Software Craftsmanship (First Edition)

by Dmytro Golodiuk

This book is a comprehensive guide for software engineers seeking to master the art and science of building robust, scalable, and maintainable systems. This book delves into the timeless principles of software engineering while integrating modern practices such as AI-augmented development, DevOps, and observability. Readers will explore essential topics including system design, architecture patterns, testing strategies, refactoring techniques, and career development insights. Whether you're an aspiring engineer or a seasoned professional, this book provides the foundational knowledge and practical skills needed to excel in today's fast-evolving tech landscape.

Published by Dmytro Golodiuk (Independently published)
For more information, visit: https://foundations.golodiuk.com
Contact: publishing@golodiuk.com

To the next generation of engineers –
may you build systems that endure,
and find joy in the craft.

Brief Contents

Contents

List of Figures

List of Tables

Acknowledgments

This book would not exist without the mentors who shaped my thinking, the colleagues who challenged my assumptions, and the mentees whose questions reminded me that clarity is earned, not given.

To my family, for their patience during the countless evenings spent writing and revising.

And to you, the reader, for choosing to invest in the foundations that will serve you throughout your career.

Part I

Preface

Chapter 1:

Letter from the Mentor: Why This Book Exists

You hold in your hands incredible power. AI can do in minutes what once took weeks. Code, architecture, tests, documentation – everything seems simpler, faster, smarter.

But I want to tell you something important: **Don't surrender completely to the temptation of instant results.**

When I started, we built systems line by line. We made mistakes, searched for causes, rewrote code, and understood. Every error taught us to think. Every line of code had meaning.

Today's world is different. AI can give you an answer immediately. But if you don't understand *why* that answer is correct, it's not knowledge. It's the illusion of knowledge.

Don't lose your **engineering thinking**. Don't let the "black box" think for you. Only those who understand principles can see when a system behaves incorrectly.

But here's what I want you to know: **mastering these principles unlocks extraordinary capability.** Engineers who understand systems don't just build faster – they build systems that adapt, scale, and endure. They see patterns others miss. They prevent failures before they happen. They turn complexity into clarity.

You can become that engineer. Not by racing through tutorials or copying AI-generated code, but by building genuine understanding – one principle at a time.

Remember these foundations:

- **AI is an amplifier, not a replacement.** If you're strong, it makes you stronger. If you're weak, it leads you faster into a dead end.
- **Speed doesn't equal progress.** Progress is when you understand *what exactly you're building and why*.
- **Always keep the system's picture in your mind.** Architecture isn't a diagram. It's a way of thinking about interaction, responsibility, and trade-offs.

So don't be afraid to think slowly. Don't be afraid to ask questions even when the answer is already "generated."

Don't be afraid to doubt – that's where the real engineer is born.

The future doesn't belong to those who simply know how to use AI. The future belongs to those who **understand how systems think**.

This book is your guide through this transformation.

In the pages ahead, you'll discover:

- How to **think like a system architect**, not just a code generator
- The **core engineering pillars** – lifecycle management, security, observability, architecture, and reliability – plus the essential human dimensions of data stewardship and collaborative culture
- How to **collaborate with AI** while maintaining engineering judgment and critical thinking
- How to **build systems that are comprehensible, observable, and evolvable** – not just functional

This is not another "DevOps handbook" or "coding manual." It's a manifesto for thoughtful engineering – a guide to help you build systems, habits, and a career that endures beyond any single technology trend.

The future doesn't belong to those who simply know how to use AI. The future belongs to those who understand how systems think – and tools change, but principles don't.

Welcome to your journey from coder to engineer.

Dmytro Golodiuk

December 2025

Chapter 2:

From Code to Systems: The Evolution of Engineering Thinking

We live at a moment when the very essence of the programmer's profession is changing. Just a few years ago, the main thing was to **write code**. Now – it's to **manage the process of its creation**.

Large Language Models (LLMs) and agentic AI systems – tools that can generate code, suggest architectures, and even autonomously execute development tasks – are transforming how software gets built. They're no longer just helpers – they're participants in the process. For experienced engineers, this is natural evolution (they have the foundation: understanding of architecture, patterns, and trade-offs). For beginners, it's a revolution.

New professionals learn not through writing code, but through **conversation with intelligence**. The risk is that you can quickly get a result – without understanding *why* it's correct.

The paradigm has shifted – from "writing" to "orchestrating."

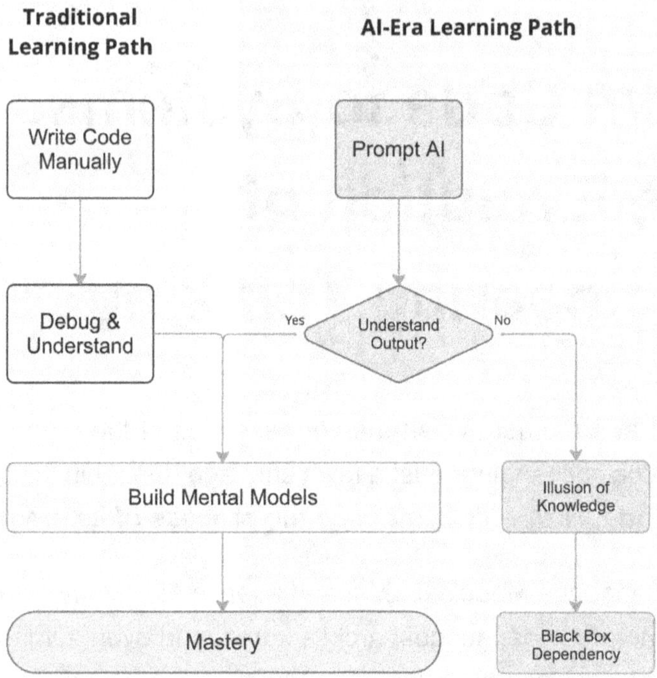

Figure 2.1: Evolution of engineering thinking – from manual code writing to AI-orchestrated development workflows

Earlier, an engineer's core skill was the ability to **write code**: knowing syntax, algorithms, patterns, and frameworks.

Now, with powerful LLMs and agentic AI, the focus shifts to **managing the code creation process**. This means:

1. **Decomposition:** Breaking down large, complex problems into clear, manageable subtasks that can be delegated to an AI agent (or a junior developer using AI).
2. **Verification:** Quickly and effectively checking AI-provided results. The question is no longer just "does the code work?" but "is it optimal, secure, and aligned with the overall architecture?"
3. **Integration:** Combining pieces of AI-generated code into a unified working system.

Chapter 3:

The AI-Augmented Era: Tools Change, Principles Don't

3.1 Why Experienced Engineers Adapt Easily

Senior and Lead engineers adapt to AI-augmented development with surprising ease. Why?

They've already done this. A senior engineer's work never consisted of simply "writing code." It always involved architecture, code review, mentorship, and decomposition. AI tools have simply become incredibly powerful "assistants" for them.

They have a mental model. Experienced developers have a clear picture in their minds of what the system *should look like*. They use AI to generate routine tasks (boilerplate code, tests, simple functions) while keeping their hands on the "steering wheel" of architecture.

Code intuition. They can look at AI-generated code and instantly sense something's wrong – even when the code is formally correct. This intuition comes only with years of experience.

> **Note**
>
> This is why the book emphasizes principles over tools. Principles give you the intuition to know when something is right or wrong, regardless of who – or what – generated it.

3.2 The Challenge for Young Professionals

For newcomers, **junior developers** and beginners face a genuinely complex and "non-obvious" situation. They face unique risks:

1. The Black Box Risk

This is the biggest danger. A junior developer can feed a problem to an LLM, get a finished piece of code, and it might even work. But the developer **doesn't understand why it works**. They haven't gone through the painful but necessary process of debugging, finding errors, and understanding basic principles.

> **Warning**
>
> Without this fundamental understanding, at the first non-standard error (or when AI "hallucinates"), such a specialist will be helpless.

2. The Illusion of Rapid Progress

AI allows beginners to create in days what used to take months (for example, a simple web application). This creates a false sense of competence. In reality, they're learning **AI operation** (prompt engineering), not **programming**.

3. Lack of Foundation for Verification

To effectively *verify* AI's work, you need to know the basics even better than before. If you don't know what asynchrony or SQL injection are, you can't evaluate whether AI generated efficient and secure code for database operations.

3.3 The Engineer's Mandate: Responsibility in the Age of AI

With this evolution comes profound **responsibility**. Engineers who orchestrate AI aren't absolved of consequences – they're more accountable than ever. You own the security vulnerabilities in generated code. You answer for system failures. You bear the ethical weight of automation decisions.

The essential skills have fundamentally shifted. The emphasis moves from memorizing syntax to:

Critical thinking and skepticism. The ability to question AI results rather than trust them at face value.

Systems thinking. Understanding not just how to write a function, but where it should live, what data it should accept and return, and how it interacts with the rest of the system.

Mastery of task formulation. The ability to formulate technical tasks – for AI or another engineer – so clearly and completely that the result is predictable.

The engineer's role evolves. From a craftsman who manually creates each part to a master who orchestrates automated tooling and robotic production lines (AI agents), controls quality, and assembles the final product.

For beginners, this means being **twice as disciplined**: use AI as an assistant for learning, but force yourself to dig deep and understand the fundamentals, even when there's temptation to simply copy ready-made solutions.

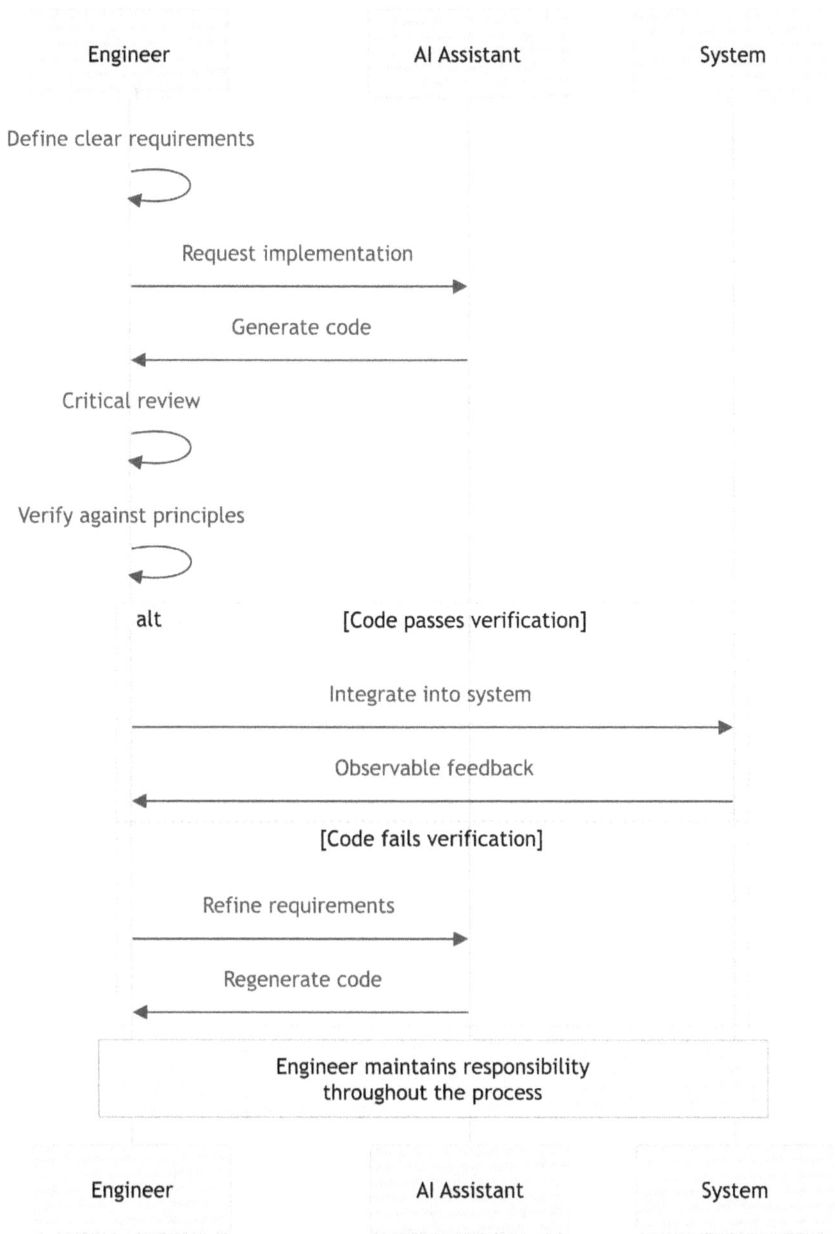

Figure 3.1: Engineer's mandate in AI era – shift from syntax memorization to critical thinking, systems reasoning, and precise task formulation

Part II

The Mindset of a Modern Engineer

Chapter 4:

From Coder to System Thinker

Have you ever fixed a bug only to watch three new ones appear somewhere else? That is the trap of coding in isolation. The function you corrected was "right," but the system behaved worse. The lesson is not that you wrote bad code – it is that you optimized the wrong thing.

This chapter is your first step in moving from writing code to shaping systems. You shift from focusing on a single line to understanding how lines connect, interact, and evolve. Tools change. Principles do not.

4.1 The Coder's Tunnel Vision

A coder is like a bricklayer focused on a single brick – meticulous, fast, even elegant – yet blind to the curve of the wall.

Tunnel vision appears when you optimize locally. A local optimization is an improvement that makes one part look better while degrading the whole. Think of a function that runs faster but returns data in a slightly different shape, breaking three downstream consumers.

> **Warning**
>
> Local fixes that ignore upstream contracts (shared API or type expectations) and downstream consumers create hidden system debt. The result is fragility that surfaces under pressure.

What breaks when you only see your code:

- Inputs and outputs lose consistency across boundaries.
- Invariants (things that must always be true) erode silently.
- Feedback loops go dark because logging and metrics were not considered.

So what changes when you widen your field of view? You start thinking in systems.

4.2 Systems Thinking in Engineering

Engineering is chess, not checkers: every move shapes the whole board. Systems thinking is looking for relationships and consequences, not just steps and syntax. It underpins the Architecture, Reliability, and Observability pillars. You notice coupling (how tightly components depend on each other), define clear boundaries, and design for change.

> **Tip**
>
> A systems thinker traces the path from requirement to production impact, making feedback loops visible.

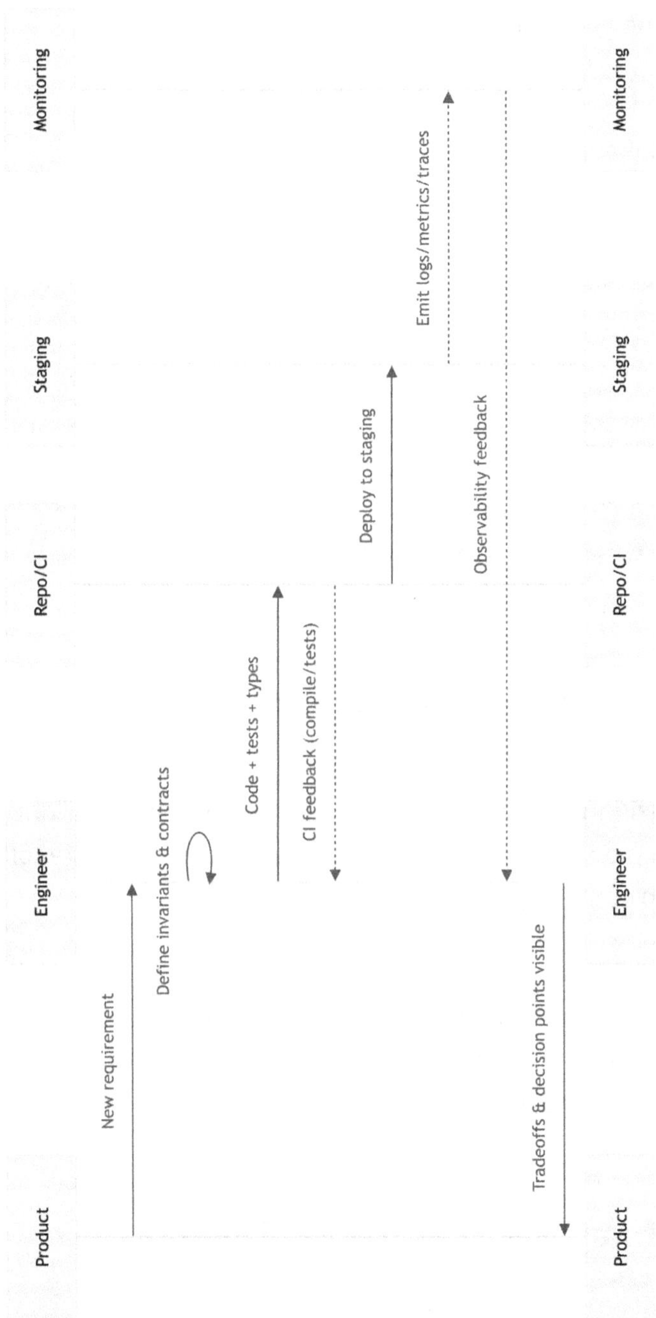

Figure 4.1: Systems thinking visualization – from tunnel vision on isolated code to understanding relationships, boundaries, and system-wide consequences

Key shifts you make:

- Make behavior explicit and observable.
- Handle failure modes with backoff, timeouts, and transparency.
- Protect invariants and contracts across the system.

> **Note**
>
> An invariant is a property that should remain true across operations (e.g., "order totals never go negative"). Protect invariants where they are easiest to enforce.

4.3 Tools Change, Principles Do Not

Memorizing a dashboard does not make you a good driver. You learn to drive by understanding friction, distance, and reaction time – principles that apply to any car.

Software works the same way. Focus on principles: contracts, boundaries, idempotency (repeating a request has the same result), observability, and resilience. These guide decisions regardless of language, framework, or trend.

4.4 Example 1: Local vs. Systemic Fix

We want a queue that preserves order while preventing duplicate users.

4.4.1 A local "fix" that harms the system

```
# Intent: Demonstrate a local optimization that breaks
↪  a system-level property (order).
from typing import List

def add_user_local(queue: List[str], user: str) ->
↪  List[str]:
    # Looks clever: remove duplicates by converting to
    ↪  a set
    # Sets are unordered; converting to a set discards
    ↪  original ordering and harms downstream
    ↪  consumers
    return list(set(queue + [user]))

q1 = ["amy", "ben", "cara"]
q1 = add_user_local(q1, "ben")  # duplicate
print(q1)  # Order may be scrambled; downstream
↪  consumers relying on order can break
```

4.4.2 A systemic fix that protects invariants

```
# Intent: Preserve both uniqueness and ordering; make
↪  the invariant explicit and cheap to verify.
from typing import List

def add_user_systemic(queue: List[str], user: str) ->
↪  List[str]:
    if user not in queue:
        queue.append(user)
    return queue

def is_valid_queue(queue: List[str]) -> bool:
    # Invariant: order preserved; no duplicates
```

```
    return len(queue) == len(set(queue))

q2 = ["amy", "ben", "cara"]
q2 = add_user_systemic(q2, "ben")  # duplicate
↪  ignored, order preserved
assert is_valid_queue(q2)
print(q2)  # ["amy", "ben", "cara"]
# Note: add_user_systemic mutates the original list
↪  (in-place update). This is intentional for
↪  simplicity.
# It prevents new duplicates; it does not remove
↪  duplicates already present in the queue.
```

Why this matters: The local fix changed a property that the rest of the system depended on (ordering). The systemic fix makes the invariant explicit and cheap to validate.

4.5 Example 2: Dependency Mapping and Type Contracts

Changing a type in one module can ripple into others. A local "any" cast masks the break now and causes failures later at runtime. A systemic fix centralizes contracts and lets the compiler reveal all affected dependencies.

4.5.1 A local "fix" that hides the problem

```
// Intent: Show how an 'any' cast hides breakage and
↪  pushes risk to runtime.
type AddressV1 = { street: string; city: string;
↪  postalCode: string };
```

```
function formatLabel(addr: AddressV1): string {
    return `${addr.street}, ${addr.city}
    ↪  ${addr.postalCode}`;
}

// Upstream change: postalCode -> zip (breaking
↪  change)
const incoming: any = { street: "1 Main St", city:
↪  "Springfield", zip: "12345" };

// Local fix: cast to any to appease compiler (bad)
console.log(formatLabel(incoming as any)); //
↪  Compiles, but will be undefined at runtime
// Output: "1 Main St, Springfield undefined"
```

4.5.2 A systemic fix with shared contracts

```
// Intent: Centralize the contract and let the
↪  compiler reveal the ripple.
// domain.ts
export type Address = { street: string; city: string;
↪  postalCode: string };
// If renamed to `zip` here, compiler errors would
↪  surface in all consumers (early warning of
↪  contract drift)

// labeler.ts
import type { Address } from "./domain";
export function formatLabel(addr: Address): string {
    return `${addr.street}, ${addr.city}
    ↪  ${addr.postalCode}`;
}

// main.ts
```

```
import { formatLabel } from "./labeler";
import type { Address } from "./domain";

// Upstream must conform to the shared contract or
↪   update it centrally
const input: Address = { street: "1 Main St", city:
↪   "Springfield", postalCode: "12345" };
console.log(formatLabel(input));
```

Why this matters: Centralized contracts turn implicit dependencies into explicit ones. The compiler becomes your early warning system.

> ⚠ Warning
>
> Small local changes can propagate into incidents without shared contracts.

4.6 Practical Habits to Grow Systems Thinking

- State invariants early. Write a one-line comment: "This function preserves X, forbids Y."
- Prefer explicit contracts (types, schemas) over implicit ones.
- Make behaviors observable. Log when a fallback triggers, including the reason and a correlation ID (an identifier that ties related logs across services), not just that it happened.
- Design for failure: use timeouts, retries with backoff, and idempotency.
- Use reviews to discuss system impact, not only code style.

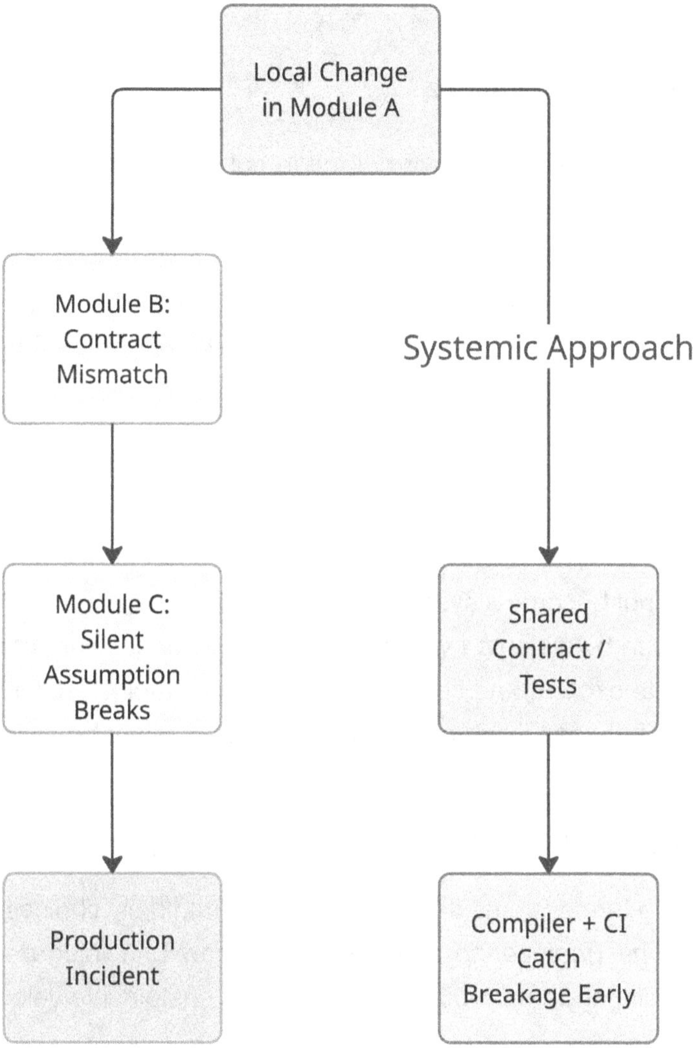

Figure 4.2: Ripple effect of contract changes – local modifications cascading into production incidents versus systemic contract enforcement catching breaks early

4.7 Self-Check

Note

Reflection Questions

- Why is writing "correct" code not enough to be a great engineer?
- Where could a local optimization harm system behavior in a project you are working on?
- What is one invariant and one contract you can make explicit this week?

4.8 Conclusion

You do not become a system thinker by writing more code – you become one by widening your field of view. Protect invariants, make contracts explicit, and keep the system observable. That is the difference between fixing bugs and designing resilient behavior.

In short: Think in systems – make behavior observable, protect invariants, and centralize contracts to prevent ripple effects.

Next, we turn systems thinking into disciplined daily choices. *Chapter 5 (The Engineering Mindset)* shows how principled decisions, guardrails, and reversibility turn clarity into sustainable velocity.

Chapter 5:

The Engineering Mindset

In *Chapter 4 (From Coder to System Thinker)*, we learned to see software as interconnected systems rather than isolated functions. Now we explore the **mindset** that guides decisions within those systems: how to choose, ship, and evolve with discipline.

Engineering is disciplined decision-making under constraints. The **Engineering Mindset** is the difference between reacting to tasks and deliberately shaping systems that remain understandable and changeable. Speed without judgment decays; disciplined speed compounds.

5.1 A Tale of Two Teams

Two teams ship the same feature. Team A hacks it in a week: no tests, no flags, no documentation. Velocity looks great – until bugs force manual patches, confidence drops, and every change feels unsafe. Team B spends two extra days clarifying assumptions, adding a feature flag, writing fast unit tests, and defining a rollback. Their first release is slightly later, but subsequent iterations are smooth, predictable, and faster overall. The lesson: unmanaged speed is noise; structured speed is signal.

> **Note**
>
> The Engineering Mindset treats every change as an investment: you evaluate cost, risk, reversibility, and long-term impact before committing.

5.2 Precision, Curiosity, Responsibility

Think like a pilot: preflight checks (precision), weather scan and alternate routes (curiosity), passenger safety (responsibility).

5.2.1 Precision

Precision means clearly framing the problem: what outcome, constraints, and success signals? You explicitly list assumptions and unknowns. A precise problem statement reduces misalignment and prevents premature optimization.

For example, "make the API faster" is vague. Precision asks: *Faster for which endpoint? Under what load? What's the current p95 latency? What's acceptable? What can we measure to confirm success?* This clarity prevents solving the wrong problem.

Define a term the first time you use it: a **guardrail** is any lightweight mechanism (tests, feature flags, monitoring) that safely constrains change. Guardrails accelerate by preventing rework. We'll explore guardrails in depth across *Chapter 10 (Pillar 1 – Lifecycle Management)*, *Chapter 11 (Pillar 2: Security)*, and *Chapter 12 (Pillar 3 Observability – Building Systems You Can See and Understand)* pillars.

5.2.2 Curiosity

Curiosity asks: "What would break? How would we know? What is the simplest reversible path?" Curiosity exposes failure modes early and turns surprises into learning rather than crisis.

For example, before deploying a caching layer, curiosity prompts: *What happens if the cache is stale? How do we detect drift between cache and source? Can we roll back to direct database calls if latency spikes? What metrics signal problems?* These questions surface risks before they become incidents.

5.2.3 Responsibility

Responsibility is owning downstream effects. You consider maintainers, operators, and users. You avoid local optimization that harms systemic stability. Responsible decisions minimize hidden coupling and maximize clarity.

For instance, changing a JSON response field from `user_id` to `userId` might simplify your code, but responsibility asks: *Who consumes this API? Will mobile apps crash? Do we have a versioning strategy? Can we deprecate the old field gracefully?* Responsible decisions account for the ripple effect.

> ⚠ Warning
>
> Precision without curiosity can yield brittle overconfidence; curiosity without responsibility can create endless exploration with no delivery.

5.2.4 The Decision Discipline Loop

Below is a compact flow of disciplined decision-making that synthesizes precision (explicit framing), curiosity (option generation), and responsibility (impact assessment). See the Figure 5.1 **Decision Discipline Loop**.

> Note
>
> The loop encodes curiosity (options), responsibility (impact assessment), and precision (explicit framing).

5.3 Reasoning About Trade-offs

Like personal budgeting: you cannot simultaneously maximize savings, luxury, and spontaneity. Every technical choice involves **trade-offs** and opportunity cost. Explicit trade-off reasoning prevents accidental complexity.

Key questions:

1. What are the primary objectives (e.g., latency, reliability, learning speed)?
2. What constraints (time, cost, skill, compliance) limit options?
3. Is this a **reversible decision** (two-way door) or an **irreversible decision** (one-way door)?
4. What guardrails mitigate risk of the chosen path?

You bias toward exploring cheaper reversible options first. For irreversible choices (e.g., selecting a database that shapes the data model for years), you invest more in evaluation – benchmarks, spike prototypes, peer review.

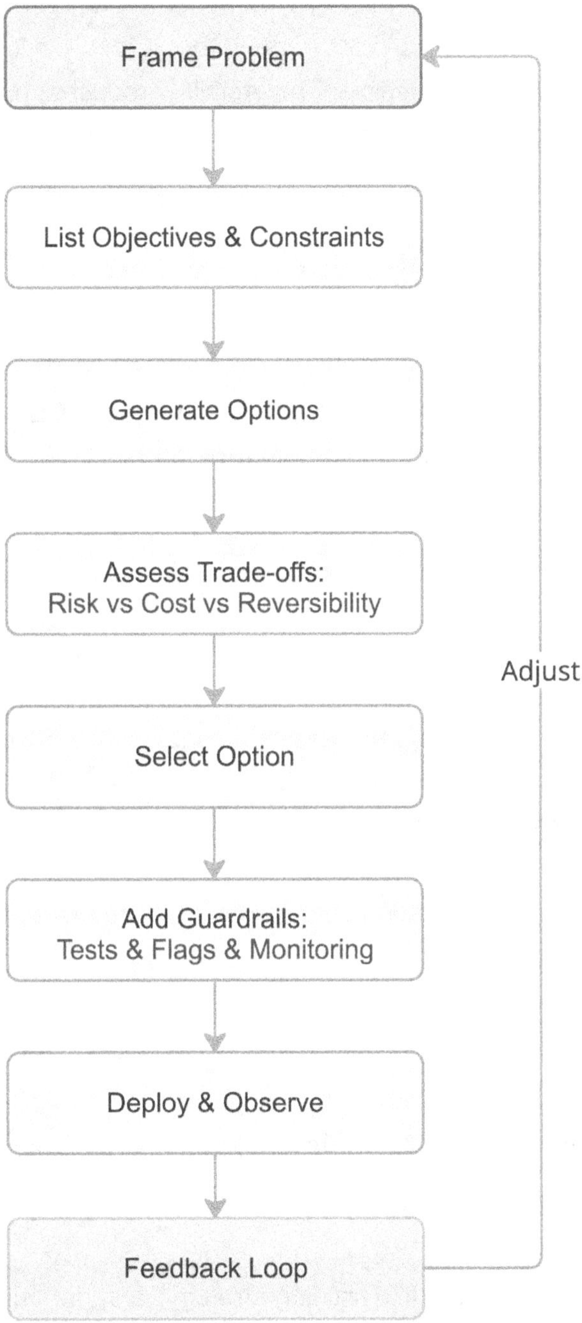

Figure 5.1: Decision discipline loop – integrating precision (framing), curiosity (options), and responsibility (impact) into a repeatable engineering workflow

> **Note**
>
> Explicitly labeling decision reversibility reduces paralysis: most choices are changeable; treat them proportionally.

5.4 Balancing Speed with Quality

"Slow is smooth, smooth is fast."

Sustainable speed emerges from reducing thrash. **Guardrails** like **automated tests**, **linting**, and **feature flags** shrink the cost of change and allow frequent small releases.

Practical tactics:

- Limit work in progress; finish and integrate before starting new streams.
- Ship behind flags; progressively enable while observing metrics.
- Write tests closest to logic risk hotspots first (critical pure functions, validation boundaries).
- Prefer instrumentation over speculation: measure before tuning.

Quality is not gold plating; it is removing friction from future change.

5.5 Managing Technical Debt: The Marathon vs The Sprint

Think of technical debt like training strategy: a sprint burns energy fast but cannot sustain distance. A marathon paces effort, managing energy as a renewable resource. Unmanaged debt is a sprint mentality applied to a marathon challenge – you deplete capacity before reaching the finish.

Technical debt is not inherently bad. Intentional debt accelerates learning; unmanaged debt accrues **technical debt interest** – the extra time spent on each future change due to shortcuts.

Principles:

- Record debt explicitly with context, impact, and an exit strategy.
- Estimate interest: added minutes/hours per change multiplied by change frequency.
- Prioritize repayment when interest exceeds new feature value.
- Make repayment incremental (e.g., refactor one module per feature cycle).

> **Note**
>
> A TODO without context is abandoned debt. A tracked item with impact and owner is managed leverage.

5.6 The Value of "Boring" Technology

Managed debt and boring technology share a philosophy: **minimize hidden costs**. Just as we track debt interest, we evaluate novelty tax – the recurring effort to understand, operate, and stabilize unfamiliar tools.

"Boring" means well-understood, battle-tested, and operable by the current team. Novel tech carries a **novelty tax** – extra time learning, integrating, and stabilizing.

Adopt novelty deliberately:

- Place innovation at the edges; keep cores stable.
- For core persistence, messaging, and authentication, prefer mature solutions unless a clear unmet requirement exists.
- Evaluate novelty tax vs differential value: does the new tool unlock a unique capability or merely cosmetic speed?
- Novelty becomes justified when it offers a **unique capability** unavailable in mature alternatives – for instance, adopting a vector database when semantic search is a core product differentiator, not cosmetic.

> ⚠ Warning
>
> Choosing novel tech on a critical path without bandwidth for deep understanding increases black box risk and instability.

5.7 Practical Applications of the Mindset

These examples illustrate reversible decisions, responsible speed via guardrails, and quantified debt – all reinforcing the decision loop above.

5.7.1 Example: Reversible Decision via Interface Seam

We create an **interface seam** for storage so initial choice is reversible.

```
// Intent: Demonstrate a reversible (two-way door)
↪  decision using a storage interface seam.
interface StoragePort {
  save(key: string, value: string): Promise<void>;
```

```
  read(key: string): Promise<string | null>;
}

class InMemoryStorage implements StoragePort {
  private data: Record<string, string> = {};
  async save(key: string, value: string) {
  ↪  this.data[key] = value; }
  async read(key: string) { return this.data[key] ??
  ↪  null; }
}

class CloudStorage implements StoragePort {
  // Placeholder for SDK integration; reversible until
  ↪  committed.
  async save(key: string, value: string) {
  ↪  console.log(`Cloud save ${key}`); }
  async read(key: string) { return null; }
}

function buildStorage(): StoragePort {
  const provider = process.env.STORAGE_PROVIDER ||
  ↪  'memory';
  if (provider === 'cloud') return new CloudStorage();
  return new InMemoryStorage();
}

async function demo() {
  const storage = buildStorage();
  await storage.save('greeting', 'hello');
  console.log(await storage.read('greeting'));
}

demo();
```

Key takeaways:

- Decision labeled reversible: we can swap implementations without refactoring callers.
- Deferred commitment: we integrate the cloud only when requirements justify it.

5.7.2 Example: Feature Flag for Responsible Speed (Python / FastAPI)

We ship behind a **feature flag** and ramp gradually while observing behavior.

```
# Intent: Ship a new endpoint behind a feature flag
↪ with progressive rollout.
from fastapi import FastAPI, Depends
import os
import random
import logging

logging.basicConfig(level=logging.INFO)
app = FastAPI()

def flag_enabled() -> bool:
    # Percentage rollout via env var
    ↪ NEW_FEATURE_PERCENT (0-100).
    pct = int(os.getenv("NEW_FEATURE_PERCENT", "0"))
    return random.randint(1, 100) <= pct

def new_feature_guard(enabled: bool =
↪ Depends(flag_enabled)):
    if not enabled:
        return False
    return True
```

```
@app.get("/stable")
def stable():
    return {"status": "ok"}

@app.get("/experimental")
def experimental(active: bool =
↪   Depends(new_feature_guard)):
    if not active:
        return {"status": "disabled"}
    logging.info("experimental feature served")
    return {"data": "new-value"}

# Run: NEW_FEATURE_PERCENT=25 uvicorn app:app --reload
```

Guardrails present:

- Controlled exposure via percentage flag.
- Logging for observation.
- Safe disabled response avoids errors.

> **Note**
>
> This example uses random rollout for simplicity. In production, use consistent hashing (e.g., based on user ID) to ensure the same user experiences stable behavior across requests, not random toggling.

5.7.3 Example: Technical Debt Register with Interest

We quantify **technical debt interest** to prioritize repayment.

```
# Intent: Sample debt register (debt_register.yaml)
- id: D1
  description: Tight coupling between payment service
↪  and email sender
  interest_minutes_per_change: 30
  change_frequency_per_week: 4
  exit_strategy: Introduce async event and decouple
↪  handlers
- id: D2
  description: Hard-coded currency conversion rates
  interest_minutes_per_change: 10
  change_frequency_per_week: 2
  exit_strategy: Externalized config + refresh job
```

```
# Intent: Compute debt interest to rank remediation
↪  priority.
import yaml
from pathlib import Path

def load_debt(path: str):
    return yaml.safe_load(Path(path).read_text())

def rank(items):
    scored = []
    for item in items:
        interest_hours =
↪  (item['interest_minutes_per_change'] / 60.0) *
↪  item['change_frequency_per_week']
        scored.append((interest_hours, item))
    return sorted(scored, key=lambda t: t[0],
     ↪  reverse=True)

if __name__ == "__main__":
    debts = load_debt("debt_register.yaml")
    for hours, item in rank(debts):
```

```
        print(f"{item['id']}: {hours:.2f} hrs/week
         ↪ interest -> {item['exit_strategy']}")
```

Interpretation: D1 costs 2.0 hours per week; if a feature delivers fewer than 2 hours of value, refactoring may yield higher ROI.

> **Note**
>
> Quantifying interest transforms debt discussions from subjective discomfort to economic reasoning.

5.8 Closing

The Engineering Mindset is a daily discipline: frame with precision, explore with curiosity, act with responsibility. Use reversible seams to postpone irreversible commitments. Apply guardrails to accelerate safely. Track technical debt like a portfolio. Prefer boring tech where reliability trumps novelty. These practices compound into sustainable velocity.

This discipline – choosing reversibility, tracking debt, preferring reliability over novelty – is **craftsmanship**. Craftsmanship is not perfectionism; it's the habit of leaving systems more understandable, more observable, and more changeable than you found them.

Next, we apply disciplined judgment with a tireless intern. *Chapter 6 (The Human – AI Collaboration)* demonstrates how to direct AI generation, verify outputs, and amplify – not replace – engineering skill.

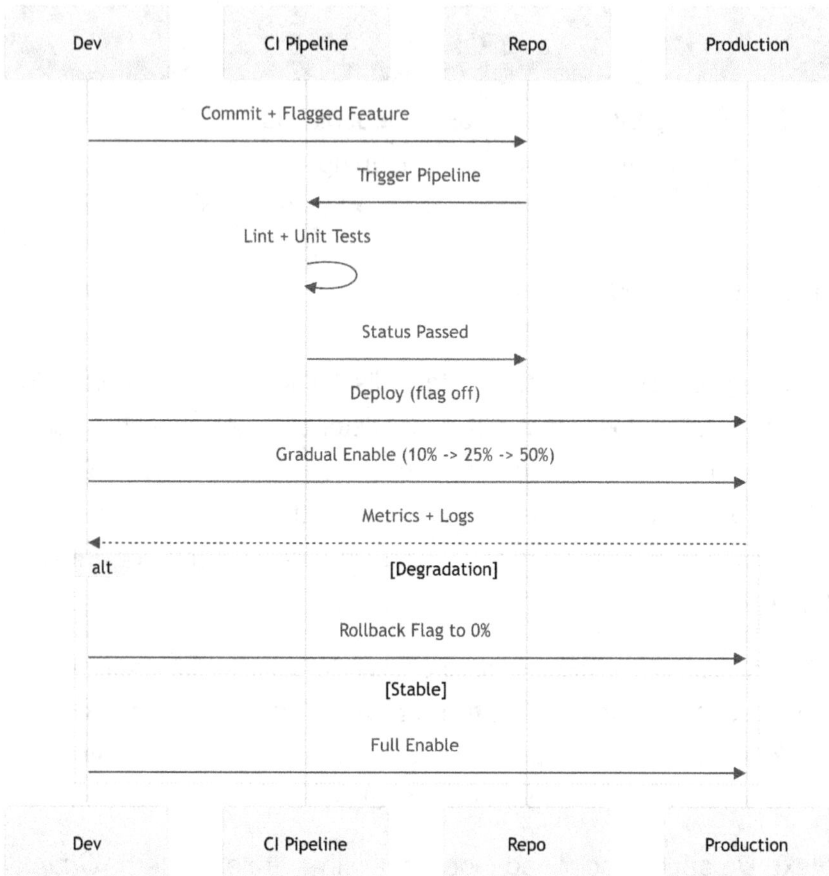

Figure 5.2: Shipping with guardrails – CI checks, feature flags, gradual enable, metrics-driven rollback or full release

Chapter 6:

The Human – AI Collaboration

In the early days of your career, you might feel a mix of excitement and anxiety about artificial intelligence (AI). Will it replace you? Will it make coding obsolete?

Consider the story of "The Copy-Paste Catastrophe." A junior engineer, eager to impress, was tasked with building a user search feature. They asked an AI assistant for the code, copied the result, and deployed it. It worked perfectly – until a user named `O'Brien` attempted to log in, causing the query to crash. Worse, a week later, a security audit revealed the code was wide open to SQL injection. The engineer had shipped code they didn't understand, assuming the machine knew better.

This chapter is about avoiding that trap. AI is not your replacement; it is your amplifier. But an amplifier makes *everything* louder – including your mistakes. To survive and thrive in this new era, you must stop being just a code writer and start being a **System Architect and Lead Reviewer**.

You are not the pilot; you are the captain. AI is your navigator.

6.1 The Co-Pilot Mindset: Active vs. Passive

The most dangerous way to use AI is as a "solution machine" – a black box where you insert a problem and extract a finished product. This is the **Passive Mindset**, and it leads to stagnation and fragile systems.

Instead, adopt the **Co-Pilot Mindset**. Treat your AI assistant like a **Tireless Intern**.

Imagine you have an intern who has read every documentation page on the internet and can type at 1,000 words per minute. However, this intern has zero real-world judgment, no understanding of your specific business context, and sometimes makes things up just to please you.

Would you push this intern's code to production without reading it? Of course not. You would review every line, ask them to explain their reasoning, and correct their mistakes.

6.1.1 The Illusion of Competence

AI models are probabilistic text generators. They are optimized to sound convincing, not necessarily to be correct. This creates an **Illusion of Competence**: the code looks clean, follows the right structure, and even includes comments. But it might be subtly wrong in ways that are hard to spot.

> ⚠ Warning
>
> You own every line of code you commit. "The AI wrote it" is never a valid excuse for a bug or a security vulnerability.

The following matrix illustrates the relationship between your skill level and your reliance on AI.

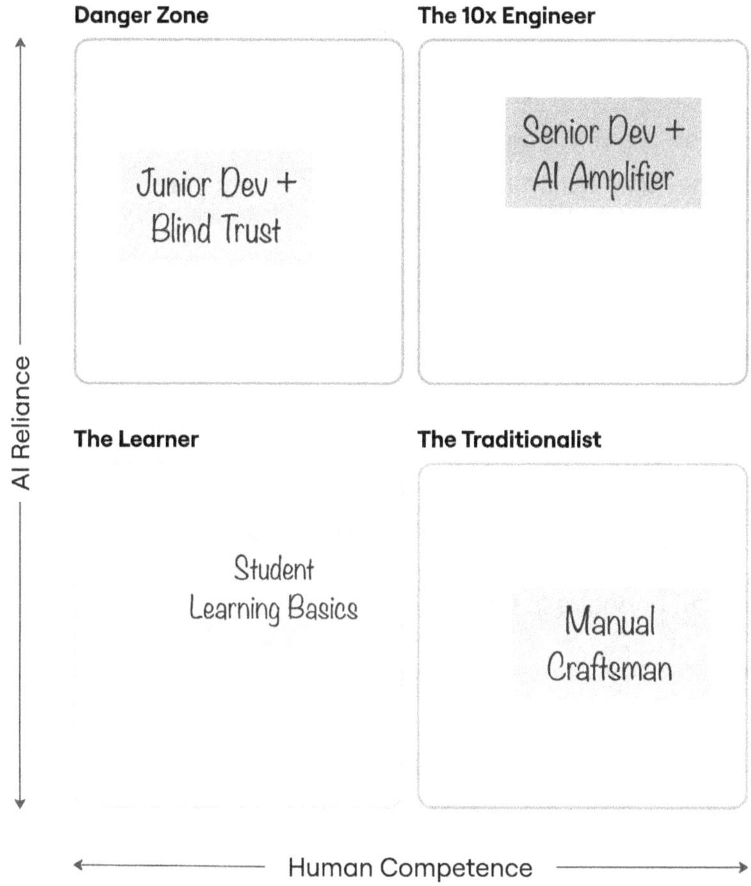

Figure 6.1: Human – AI leverage matrix – moving from passive reliance to active co-pilot: high competence paired with high AI leverage

Your goal is to move to the top right: high competence *and* high leverage. But you cannot get there by skipping the learning phase. You must understand the fundamentals to effectively direct the machine.

6.2 Prompt Engineering as Technical Specification

If you cannot articulate the problem clearly to the AI, you do not understand the problem well enough to solve it.

Think of prompt engineering as **rubber duck debugging on steroids**. In traditional debugging, explaining your problem line by line to an inanimate object often helps you find the solution yourself. With AI, that explanation becomes the specification for the solution.

6.2.1 Context is King

A vague prompt yields a generic (and often poor) answer. A specific prompt yields a tailored solution.

Bad Prompt:

"Write an endpoint to fetch an invoice by ID."

Good Prompt:

"Write a FastAPI endpoint using SQLAlchemy to fetch an invoice by ID for the authenticated user. Enforce per-tenant ownership and return 404 if not owned. Use a Pydantic response model."

6.2.2 Iterative Refinement

The first answer is rarely the best. Use AI to explore the problem space.

1. **Draft:** Ask for a solution.
2. **Critique:** Ask the AI, "Are there any security vulnerabilities in this code?" or "How would this handle a list of 1 million users?"
3. **Refine:** Ask it to rewrite the code, addressing those concerns.

6.2.3 Example: The Authorization Blind Spot

AI can produce clean, idiomatic code while missing business-context security. A common oversight is authorization. Models don't know your tenancy rules.

The Request: "Write a FastAPI endpoint to fetch an invoice by ID."

The naive AI output (insecure: no ownership check):

```
# BAD: Returns invoices across tenants; leaks data
↪  without ownership enforcement
from fastapi import APIRouter, Depends, HTTPException
from sqlalchemy.orm import Session
from .db import get_db
from .models import Invoice

router = APIRouter()

@router.get("/invoices/{invoice_id}")
def get_invoice(invoice_id: int, db: Session =
↪  Depends(get_db)):
    invoice = db.get(Invoice, invoice_id)
    if not invoice:
        raise HTTPException(status_code=404,
         ↪  detail="Invoice not found")
    return invoice
```

The engineer's correction (enforce per-tenant ownership):

```
# Secure: Enforce row-level authorization and avoid
↪  enumerating others' objects
from fastapi import APIRouter, Depends, HTTPException
from sqlalchemy.orm import Session
from sqlalchemy import select
from .db import get_db
```

```
from .auth import get_current_user
from .models import Invoice, User
from .schemas import InvoiceOut

router = APIRouter()

@router.get("/invoices/{invoice_id}",
↪   response_model=InvoiceOut)
def get_invoice(
    invoice_id: int,
    db: Session = Depends(get_db),
    current_user: User = Depends(get_current_user),
):
    """
    Enforce per-tenant access: only the owner can
↪   fetch this invoice.
    Return 404 to avoid leaking the existence of
↪   others' invoices.
    """
    invoice = db.scalar(
        select(Invoice).where(
            Invoice.id == invoice_id,
            Invoice.user_id == current_user.id,
        )
    )
    if not invoice:
        raise HTTPException(status_code=404,
         ↪ detail="Invoice not found")
    return invoice
```

Note

This pattern generalizes to projects, orders, files – anything multi-tenant. Specify and test ownership rules; AI will not infer them.

6.3 The Art of Validation: Trust but Verify

Using AI effectively requires a shift in how you spend your energy: less typing, more verifying.

Think of this as using a GPS. A GPS is an incredible tool that saves you time and mental energy. But if the GPS tells you to turn left into a lake, you don't do it. You look out the window.

6.3.1 Spotting Hallucinations

AI models can "hallucinate" – confidently inventing libraries, functions, or syntax that do not exist.

- **The Library Ghost:** The AI imports `import fast_math_lib` because it sounds plausible, but the library doesn't exist.
- **The Deprecated Method:** The AI uses a function that was removed in the latest version of the framework.

6.3.2 The "Smell Test"

Does the code feel right? Does it match the architectural style of your project?

- **Complexity:** Did the AI write 50 lines of code for something that should be a one-line library call?
- **Consistency:** Did it switch from `camelCase` to `snake_case` halfway through?

6.3.3 Example: The Scalability Trap (In-Memory vs Database)

AI optimizes for concise code, not data scale. It often fetches everything and filters in memory – fine for 100 rows, disastrous for 100,000.

The Request: "Write a TypeScript function to find users who haven't logged in for 30 days."

The Naive AI Output (In-memory filter):

```
// BAD: Loads entire table; slow and memory intensive
↪ at scale
import { prisma } from "./db";
import dayjs from "dayjs";

export async function findInactiveUsers(days: number)
↪ {
  const cutoff = dayjs().subtract(days, "day");
  const users = await prisma.user.findMany();
  return users.filter((u) =>
   ↪ dayjs(u.lastLoginAt).isBefore(cutoff));
}
```

The Engineer's Correction (DB-side filter + pagination):

```
// Scalable: push filter to DB, paginate, and select
↪ only needed fields
import { prisma } from "./db";

export async function findInactiveUsers(days: number,
↪ pageSize = 1000) {
  const cutoff = new Date(Date.now() - days * 24 * 60
   ↪ * 60 * 1000);
```

```
  const results: Array<{ id: number; email: string;
  ↪ lastLoginAt: Date | null }> = [];
  let cursor: number | undefined = undefined;

  while (true) {
    const page = await prisma.user.findMany({
      where: { lastLoginAt: { lt: cutoff } },
      select: { id: true, email: true, lastLoginAt:
↪   true },
      take: pageSize,
      ...(cursor ? { cursor: { id: cursor }, skip: 1 }
      ↪ : {}),
      orderBy: { id: "asc" },
    });
    if (page.length === 0) break;
    results.push(...page);
    cursor = page[page.length - 1].id;
  }
  return results;
}
```

> **Note**
>
> Specify performance constraints in prompts (data volume, latency budgets) and verify that filtering and ordering execute in the database.

6.3.4 The AI-Augmented Workflow

Collaboration with AI is not a linear path from question to answer; it is a cycle of refinement. To consistently produce high-quality software, you must formalize the interaction into a repeatable process.

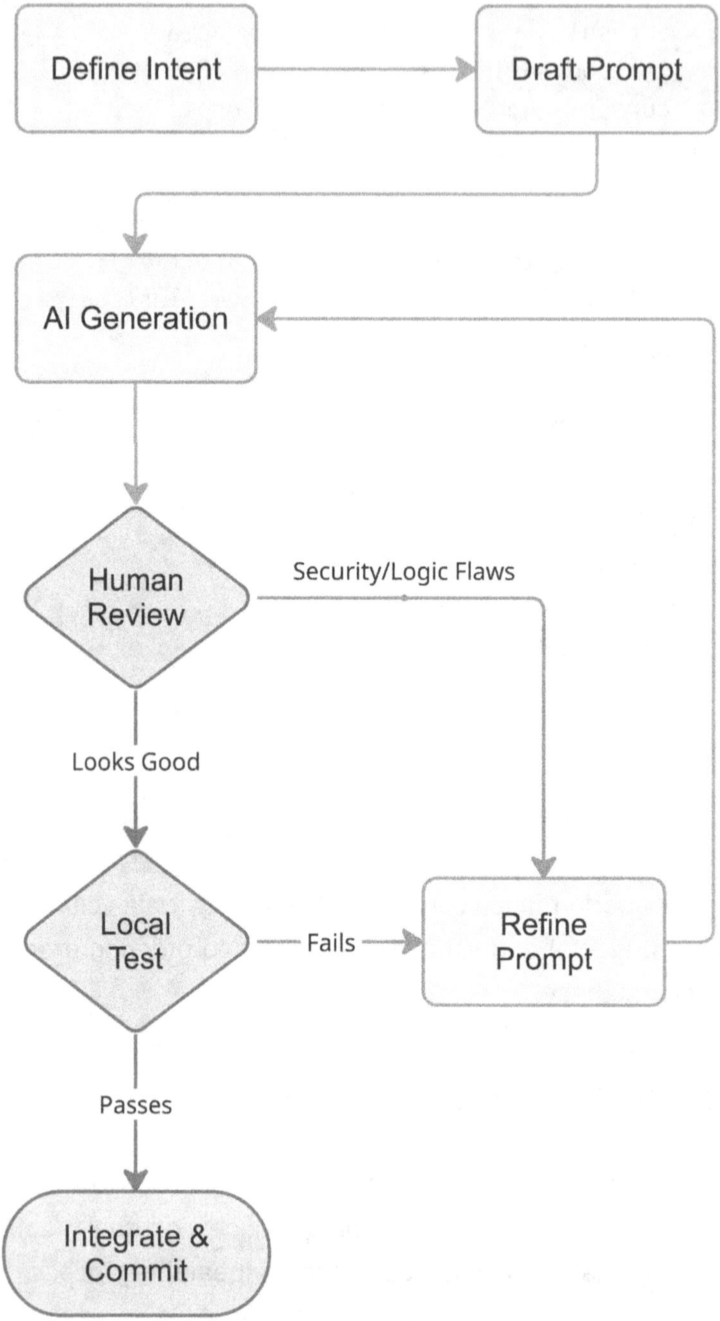

Figure 6.2: AI-augmented workflow – define intent, prompt, generate, review, test, and iterate before integration

This workflow enforces the "Co-Pilot Mindset" at every stage:

1. **Define Intent:** Before opening the chat window, clearly define what you need. Are you exploring a concept, generating boilerplate, or debugging a specific error?
2. **Prompt:** Craft a specific request with context and constraints.
3. **Generate:** Let the AI produce the draft.
4. **Review & Test:** Apply the "Smell Test" and verify against requirements. Look for security gaps and hallucinations.
5. **Iterate:** If the output is flawed, do not fix it manually immediately. Refine your prompt to guide the AI to the correct solution. This improves your prompting skills and ensures the AI context remains accurate for follow-up questions.

Only when the code passes this loop does it move to integration.

6.4 Conclusion

AI is a tool that rewards depth. The more you know about software engineering principles – security, testing, architecture – the more value you can extract from AI.

If you use AI to avoid learning, you will remain a junior engineer, dependent on a machine you don't understand. If you use AI to accelerate your learning and handle the drudgery, you become a system thinker who can build faster and better than ever before.

Next, we make collaboration tangible at the keyboard. *Chapter 7 (Code is for Humans First, Computers Second)* shows how naming, structure, and empathy turn AI-assisted output into readable, maintainable code.

Part III

The Craft of Code

Chapter 7:

Code is for Humans First, Computers Second

You finish a feature. The tests pass. The linter is happy. You merge the PR, close the ticket, and move on. Job done, right?

Six months later, a bug report appears. You open the file. You stare, squint, scroll, and finally whisper: "What was I trying to do here?"

This is the **Compiler Fallacy** – assuming that if code compiles and runs, the engineering work is complete.

In practice, professional engineering time skews heavily toward maintenance. Engineers spend roughly 10% of their time writing new code and 90% reading, debugging, and modifying existing code. Optimizing only for typing speed ("I'll just hack this in") favors the 10% at the expense of the 90%.

> **Note**
>
> The 10% / 90% split is a heuristic illustrating the imbalance between creation and maintenance. Exact ratios vary by team and domain, but the principle holds: most effort goes into understanding and evolving existing code.

Code is not just a set of instructions for a machine. It is a message to the next engineer who touches it. That engineer might be a teammate, a future hire, or – very often – you, months from now.

7.1 Code as Literature

Imagine picking up a technical manual for a complex machine, only to find cryptic shorthand, pages out of order, and critical warnings buried in the margins. You would not trust that machine.

Now imagine your code.

When you write code, you author a narrative. Readers try to answer: *What problem does this solve? How does it solve it? What are its constraints?*

If someone must reverse-engineer logic to discover intent, communication has failed.

Intent vs. Implementation

There is a difference between *what* code does (implementation) and *why* it exists (intent).

- **Implementation:** "Iterate through list `x`, check if `x[i].s` is `'A'`, then add to list `y`."
- **Intent:** "Find all active users."

Good code makes intent obvious. The reader should not have to decipher low-level mechanics. This reflects the **Principle of Least Astonishment** – code should act as a reasonable reader expects based on its name and context.

7.2 Managing Cognitive Load

Human short-term memory holds only about seven items (plus or minus two). **Cognitive load** is the mental effort required to understand and work with code.

> **Note**
>
> The classic "7 ± 2" figure comes from Miller (1956). Modern cognitive research often cites a practical working memory capacity closer to 4 ± 1 chunks. Either way, capacity is limited – so code should reduce unnecessary mental tracking.

Each variable, side effect, nested loop, or magic number occupies a slot in the reader's mental buffer. When the buffer overflows, comprehension collapses, and the reader must rebuild the model from scratch.

Think of code like a workbench:

- **Messy:** Loose screws, sawdust, three hammers, a half-eaten sandwich – work starts only after cleanup.
- **Organized:** A surgical tray with only required instruments laid out in order.

Minimize **cognitive load** so attention stays on the *business logic*, not on tracking the fate of variable `i` across nested loops.

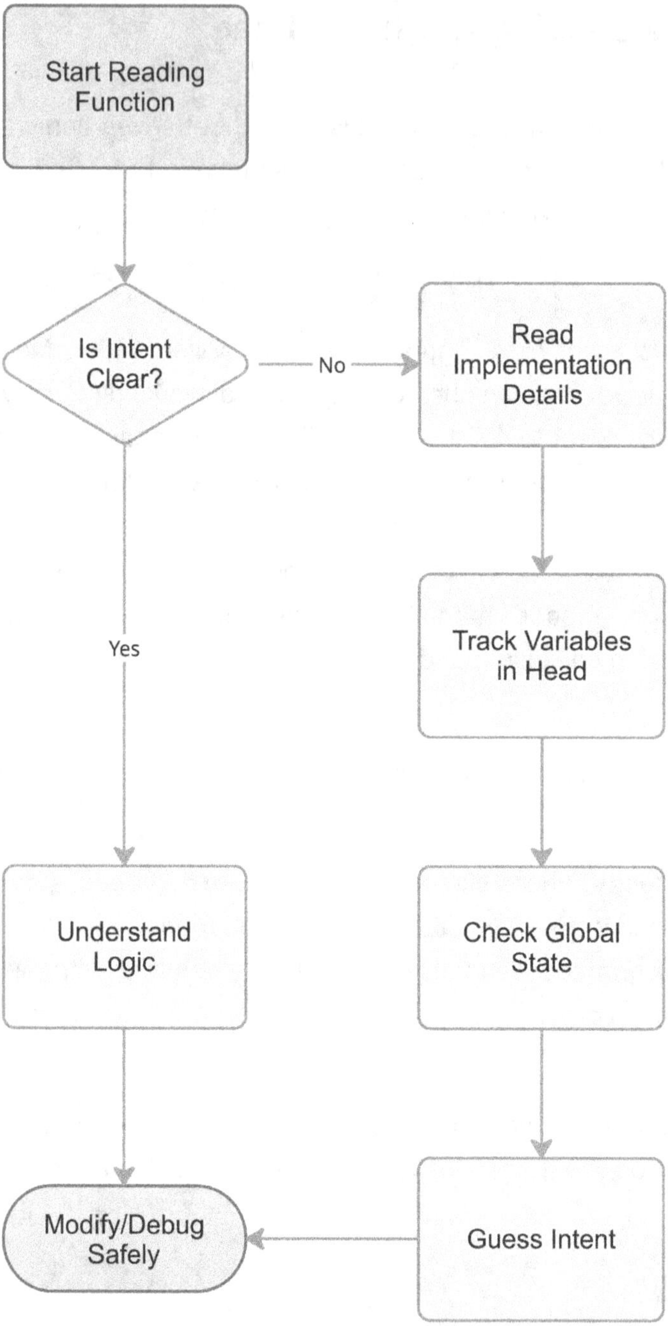

Figure 7.1: Managing cognitive load – from messy workbench to organized tray; reduce mental tracking with clear names, simple structure, and visible intent

The "Clever" Trap

Early-career engineers often mistake "cleverness" for seniority and write dense one-liners that do three things at once using obscure features.

Clever code is technical debt. If a new teammate cannot understand your "elegant" line without consulting the language spec, clarity has been sacrificed.

Example: The Cost of Cleverness (C#)

The "Clever" Way: This compact LINQ query forces the reader to unpack filtering, grouping, summation, sorting, and limiting in one breath. We also filter on `Stock > 0`, meaning only currently available products are considered.

```
// Intent: Get the top 3 best-selling in-stock
↪  products in the 'Electronics' category.
var topSellers = products.Where(p => p.Category ==
↪  "Electronics" && p.Stock > 0)
                           .GroupBy(p => p.Id)
                           .Select(g => new { Id =
                           ↪  g.Key, Total = g.Sum(x =>
                           ↪  x.Sales) })
                           .OrderByDescending(x =>
                           ↪  x.Total)
                           .Take(3)
                           .ToList();
```

The Readable Way: Breaking the query apart lets the reader verify each step. The compiler emits similar machine code; the difference is purely human comprehension.

```
// Intent: Get the top 3 best-selling in-stock
↪   products in the 'Electronics' category.
var electronics = products.Where(p => p.Category ==
↪   "Electronics" && p.Stock > 0);

var salesByProduct = electronics.GroupBy(p => p.Id)
                                .Select(g => new {
                                    ProductId = g.Key,
                                    TotalSales =
↪   g.Sum(x => x.Sales)
                                });

var topSellers = salesByProduct.OrderByDescending(x =>
↪   x.TotalSales)
                               .Take(3)
                               .ToList();
```

Just as logic can be too dense, language describing it can be too vague.

7.3 The Art of Naming

Naming is a design task, not decoration. A name defines scope and purpose.

> **Note**
>
> There are only two hard things in Computer Science: cache invalidation and naming things.

If you cannot name something clearly, you may not understand it, or it may be doing too much.

Imagine a warehouse where every box is labeled "Box 1," "Box 2," or "Stuff." You would never find anything. You need labels like "Fragile – Electronics – Aisle 4."

Rules for Naming

1. **Reveal intent:** `daysSinceCreation` is better than d or `days` .
2. **Avoid noise:** `data` , `info` , `manager` , `processor` are often filler words. `UserManager` tells you nothing. `UserAuthenticator` tells you something.
3. **Use pronounceable names:** If you cannot say it out loud, you cannot discuss it in a code review.

Example: The Transformation of Intent

Before: This code runs, but it hides business logic behind cryptic names and magic numbers.

```
# What is 'd'? What is 4? What is 0?
def get_x(l):
    x = []
    for i in l:
        if i[0] == 4:
            x.append(i)
    return x
```

After: By naming concepts, the code becomes self-documenting. We also shift from positional indexing in a tuple/list structure to a simple object with a `status` attribute – this reduces ambiguity. We do not need comments to explain *what* happens.

```
# Constants give meaning to magic numbers
STATUS_ACTIVE = 4
```

```
def get_active_users(users):
    active_users = []
    for user in users:
        if user.status == STATUS_ACTIVE:
            active_users.append(user)
    return active_users
```

7.4 Structure and "The Newspaper Metaphor"

Good code reads like a newspaper article.

1. **The Headline:** The name of the function or class. It tells you the big picture.
2. **The Lead Paragraph:** The high-level logic that orchestrates the flow.
3. **The Details:** The low-level helper functions and implementation specifics, tucked away at the bottom.

You should be able to read the "headline" and "lead" and stop if deeper details are unnecessary.

Encapsulating Complexity

One reliable way to improve structure is to hide complexity behind descriptive function calls. This follows the **Single Responsibility Principle (SRP)**: a function should have one reason to change.

Example: Encapsulating Boolean Logic

Before: The reader must parse a complex boolean expression to understand *why* execution enters the block.

```
// Supporting model definitions for clarity
interface Order { status: 'PENDING' | 'APPROVED' |
↪  'CANCELLED'; total: number; hasFraudFlag: boolean;
↪  }
interface User { isPremium: boolean; }
const HIGH_VALUE_THRESHOLD = 100;

// Complex condition mixed with business logic
if (order.status === 'PENDING' && (order.total >
↪  HIGH_VALUE_THRESHOLD || user.isPremium) &&
↪  !order.hasFraudFlag) {
    // ... process order ...
}
```

After: We extract complexity into a semantically named function. The `if` now reads like English.

```
// The condition is now a semantic question
if (canProcessOrder(order, user)) {
    processOrder(order);
}

// The complexity is encapsulated here
function canProcessOrder(order: Order, user: User):
↪  boolean {
    const isEligible = order.total >
    ↪  HIGH_VALUE_THRESHOLD || user.isPremium;
    const isSafe = order.hasFraudFlag === false; //
    ↪  explicit for clarity
    const isPending = order.status === 'PENDING';
    return isPending && isEligible && isSafe;
}
```

7.5 Conclusion: The Empathy Test

Before you commit code, pause and ask: *"If I were an engineer joining this team tomorrow, would I understand this without asking for help?"* This is the **Empathy Test**.

Writing code for computers is easy – compilers are strict yet predictable. Writing code for humans is harder – humans are busy, tired, and context-limited. But humans maintain, fix, and extend your work.

Be kind to them – and to your future self. Write code that tells a clear story.

You now know how to write code that tells a story. *Chapter 8 (The Testing Pyramid)* shows how to build a testing stack that preserves that story under change – unit focus, integration truth, and system trust.

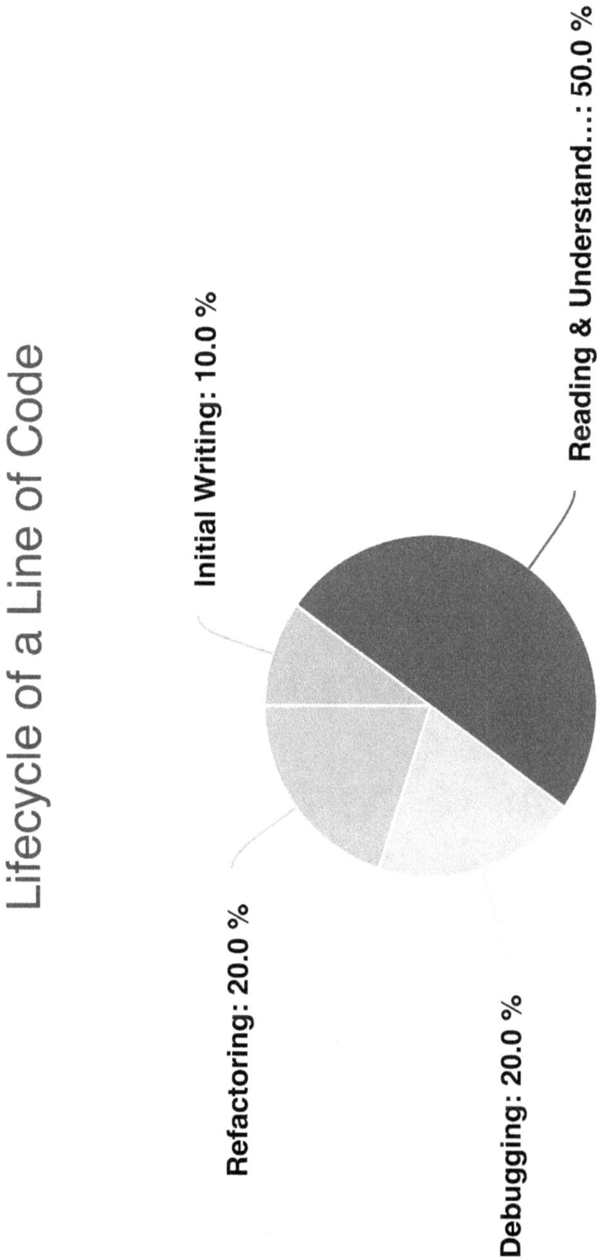

Figure 7.2: The Empathy Test – write code a new teammate can understand without hand-holding; prioritize clarity, visible intent, and simple structure over cleverness

Chapter 8:

The Testing Pyramid

Readable code, described in *Chapter 7 (Code is for Humans First, Computers Second)*, gives us intent we can trust; tested code gives us intent we can change safely. This chapter frames the **Testing Pyramid** as a risk-aligned feedback system: fast unit tests protect pure logic, integration tests verify behavior across boundaries, and a thin layer of end-to-end tests guards critical user journeys without slowing iteration.

We will avoid **cargo-cult layering** – blindly copying a structure without understanding its purpose – and instead focus on value: each test tier answers a different question about correctness, collaboration, and resilience. The goal is confidence per wall-clock minute, not accumulating test count.

> **Note**
>
> A pyramid is a shape of cost distribution, not of prestige – slow UI tests are not "better," they are just more expensive.

8.1 The Fear of the Legacy Monolith

Every engineer knows the feeling. You open a file in a legacy codebase – a 5,000-line "God Class" that handles billing, notifications, and user management. You need to modify one line to resolve a tax calculation issue. You stare at the screen, paralyzed.

If I make this change, will the user still receive their receipt? Will the admin dashboard crash? Will the database lock up?

You make the change, cross your fingers, and deploy. This is "Hope-Driven Development."

Testing is the antidote to this fear. It is not a chore for the QA department; it is a selfish act for the developer. A good test suite turns "I hope this works" into "I know this works." It is the safety net that allows you to refactor, optimize, and evolve your system without the constant dread of breaking it.

8.2 The Economics of Feedback

Why do we structure tests as a pyramid? Why not just write one big test that runs the whole app and checks everything?

Imagine a construction site:

1. **The Brick (Unit):** Before a bricklayer places a brick, they check if it is cracked. This takes one second.
2. **The Wall (Integration):** Once the wall is built, the foreman checks if it is plumb and level. This takes ten minutes.
3. **The House (End-to-End):** Once the roof is on, the inspector checks if the house is habitable. This takes a day.

If you wait until the house is finished to check the bricks, finding a cracked one means tearing down the wall. The cost of fixing a bug increases by an order of magnitude at each layer it escapes.

The **Testing Pyramid** optimizes for this economic reality. We want to catch most bugs while they are cheap (Unit), some bugs when they are connected (Integration), and a few critical bugs when the system is live (End-to-End).

While there is no "golden ratio," a healthy portfolio often resembles a **70/20/10 split**: 70% fast unit tests to cover logic, 20% integration tests to verify boundaries, and 10% broad E2E tests to validate journeys.

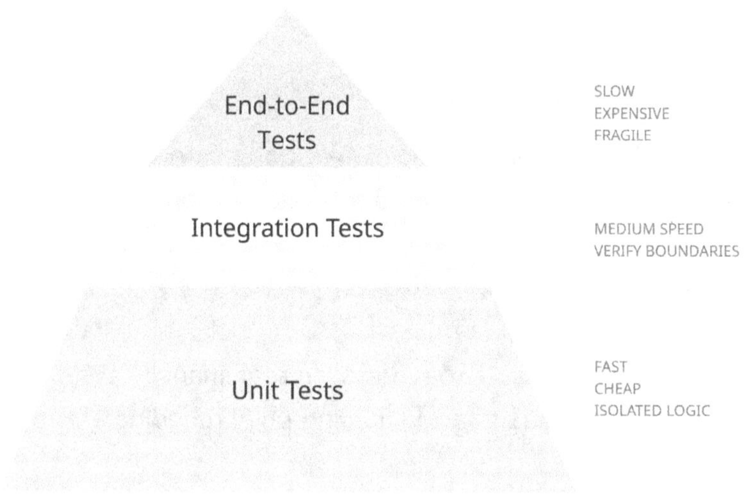

Figure 8.1: Testing Pyramid – cost-weighted distribution of Unit (base), Integration (middle), and End-to-End (peak) tests

8.3 The Base: Unit Tests (The Bricks)

The base of the pyramid is built of **Unit Tests**. These are your first line of defense.

A unit test verifies a small, isolated piece of logic – a single function, a class, or a module – without any external dependencies. No databases, no network calls, no file systems. Because they are isolated, they are **fast**. You should be able to run thousands of them in seconds.

Characteristics:

- **Fast:** Sub-millisecond execution.
- **Deterministic**: Always returns the same result for the same input.
- **Isolated:** Mocks or stubs all dependencies.

Example: The Discount Calculator

Here, we test pure business logic. We don't care where the cart comes from or how the result is displayed. We only care that the math is correct.

> **Note**
>
> For simplicity, we use `float` here. In real financial systems, always use `Decimal` to avoid floating-point rounding errors.

```
# discount_calculator.py
class DiscountCalculator:
    def calculate(self, total: float, is_vip: bool) ->
    ↪   float:
        """Calculates final price with VIP rules."""
```

```
        if total < 0:
            raise ValueError("Total cannot be
             ↪  negative")

        discount = 0.0
        if total > 100:
            discount = 0.10

        if is_vip:
            discount += 0.05

        return total * (1 - discount)

# test_discount_calculator.py
import unittest
from discount_calculator import DiscountCalculator

class TestDiscountCalculator(unittest.TestCase):
    def setUp(self):
        self.calculator = DiscountCalculator()

    def test_apply_standard_discount_over_100(self):
        # Intent: Verify 10% discount for orders >
         ↪  $100
        result = self.calculator.calculate(150.0,
 ↪  is_vip=False)
        self.assertEqual(result, 135.0)

    def test_apply_vip_bonus(self):
        # Intent: Verify VIPs get an extra 5% (total
         ↪  15% if > $100)
        result = self.calculator.calculate(150.0,
 ↪  is_vip=True)
        self.assertEqual(result, 127.5)
```

```
    def test_negative_total_raises_error(self):
        # Intent: Ensure invalid inputs are rejected
        ↪   immediately
        with self.assertRaises(ValueError):
            self.calculator.calculate(-10.0,
            ↪   is_vip=False)
```

8.4 The Middle: Integration Tests (The Wiring)

Unit tests tell you that your components work in isolation. **Integration Tests** tell you if they work *together*.

Think of a lamp and a wall socket. The lamp works (you tested the bulb). The socket works (you tested the voltage). But does the plug fit the socket? That is an integration test.

These tests verify the **boundaries** of your system:

- Does my code save to the database correctly?
- Does my service parse the API response from the payment gateway correctly?

Characteristics:

- **Slower:** Involves I/O (database, network).
- **Broader Scope:** Tests the interaction between two or more units.
- **Real Dependencies:** Often uses a real (test) database or a Docker container, not just mocks.

Example: The User Repository

Here, we don't care about the business logic of *why* a user is created. We care about the *contract* with the database: if we send this object, does it actually persist?

```
// user.repository.ts
import { Pool } from 'pg';

export class UserRepository {
  constructor(private db: Pool) {}

  async create(username: string, email: string):
  ↪  Promise<number> {
    const result = await this.db.query(
      'INSERT INTO users (username, email) VALUES ($1,
      ↪  $2) RETURNING id',
      [username, email]
    );
    return result.rows[0].id;
  }
}

// user.repository.test.ts
// Assumes a test runner like Jest or Vitest
import { Pool } from 'pg';
import { UserRepository } from './user.repository';

describe('UserRepository Integration', () => {
  let pool: Pool;
  let repo: UserRepository;

  beforeAll(async () => {
    // Setup connection to a test database container
```

```
    pool = new Pool({ connectionString: process.env.TEST_DB_URL });
    repo = new UserRepository(pool);
    // In a real scenario, you would run migrations here to ensure the 'users' table exists
  });

  afterAll(async () => {
    await pool.end();
  });

  it('should persist a new user to the database', async () => {
    // Intent: Verify the SQL query actually works against a real DB schema
    const userId = await repo.create('testuser', 'test@example.com');
    const result = await pool.query('SELECT * FROM users WHERE id = $1', [userId]);

    expect(result.rows).toHaveLength(1);
    expect(result.rows[0].username).toBe('testuser');
  });
});
```

> **Note**
>
> Do not test the framework. You don't need to test that PostgreSQL works; you need to test that *your query* matches your schema.

8.5 The Peak: End-to-End Tests (The Test Drive)

At the top of the pyramid are **End-to-End (E2E) Tests**. These simulate a real user interacting with your application. A robot opens a browser, clicks "Login," adds an item to the cart, and clicks "Checkout."

These tests give you the highest confidence because they exercise the entire stack – frontend, backend, database, and network. However, they come with a high price tag.

Characteristics:

- **Slow:** Can take minutes to run.
- **Fragile**: If you rename a CSS class or move a button, the test breaks even if the logic is fine.
- **Expensive:** Hard to debug when they fail.

Example: The Critical Path (Playwright/TypeScript)

Here, we act as the user. We don't know about the database or the `DiscountCalculator` class. We only know about buttons and URLs.

```
// checkout.spec.ts
import { test, expect } from '@playwright/test';

test('User can complete a purchase', async ({ page })
↪  => {
  // 1. Login
  await page.goto('/login');
  await page.fill('#username', 'testuser');
  await page.fill('#password', 'securepass');
```

```
  await page.click('button[type="submit"]');

  // 2. Add to cart
  await page.click('text=Premium Widget');
  await page.click('#add-to-cart');

  // 3. Checkout
  await page.click('#cart-icon');
  await page.click('#checkout-button');

  // Intent: Verify the user actually sees the success
  ↪  message
  await expect(page.locator('.order-confirmation'))
        .toContainText('Thank you for your order');
});
```

Use E2E tests sparingly. Focus on **Critical User Journeys** – the paths that, if broken, mean you lose money or trust immediately (e.g., Login, Signup, Checkout).

> **Further Reading**
>
> See *Chapter 12 (Pillar 3 Observability – Building Systems You Can See and Understand)* for the Golden Signals and synthetic probes that continuously validate user journeys. See *Chapter 14 (Pillar 5 – Reliability and Resilience)* for resilience patterns (timeouts, retries, circuit breakers, bulkheads) that keep those journeys reliable under stress.

8.6 What Not to Test

Knowing what *not* to test is as important as knowing what to test. Avoid the trap of 100% coverage for the sake of vanity metrics.

1. **The Framework:** Do not test that React renders a `div` or that Django saves a model. Trust the library authors. Test *your* logic, not theirs.
2. **Trivial Getters/Setters:** Testing `def get_x(self): return self.x` adds maintenance weight with zero safety value.
3. **Implementation Details:** Do not test private methods directly. If you refactor a private helper method, your tests should not break as long as the public behavior remains the same.

8.7 The Maintenance Trap: Tests Rot Too

Tests are code. They require maintenance, refactoring, and care. A test suite that is hard to read or constantly fails (flaky tests) becomes technical debt.

> **Note**
>
> This connects directly to *Chapter 14 (Pillar 5 – Reliability and Resilience)*. A flaky test suite destroys trust in the deployment pipeline, forcing teams back into manual verification.

Test Behavior, Not Implementation.

If you rename a variable inside a function and 50 tests break, your tests are too coupled to the implementation. Good tests treat the system as a black box: “If I give you X, do you return Y?”

8.8 The Anti-Pattern: The Ice Cream Cone

When teams ignore these ratios and rely too heavily on manual or E2E verification, they invert the pyramid.

Many teams accidentally build the **Ice Cream Cone**: a huge scoop of manual and E2E tests balancing precariously on a tiny cone of unit tests.

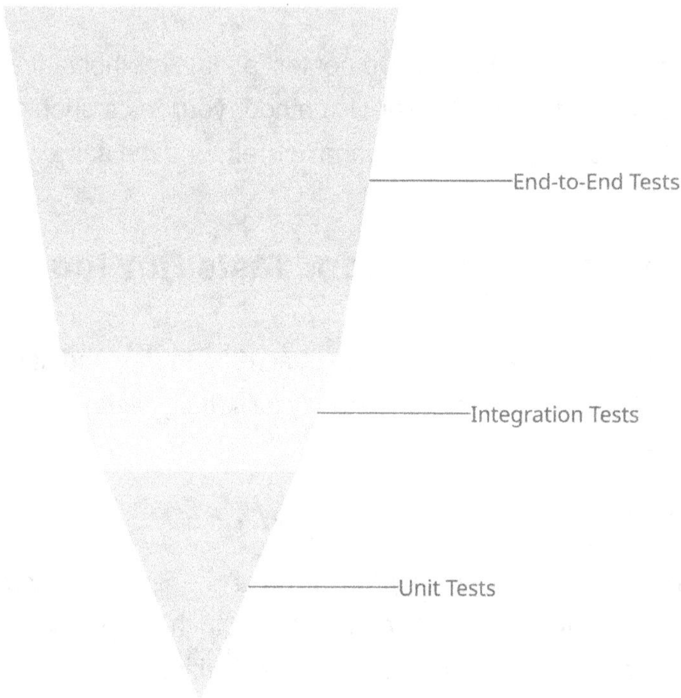

Figure 8.2: Ice Cream Cone anti-pattern – heavy manual/E2E tests balancing on a tiny unit base

When you rely on slow tests, the feedback loop lengthens. You commit code, wait 30 minutes for the build, see a failure, and have to context-switch back to fix it. This friction kills productivity and encourages developers to skip testing altogether.

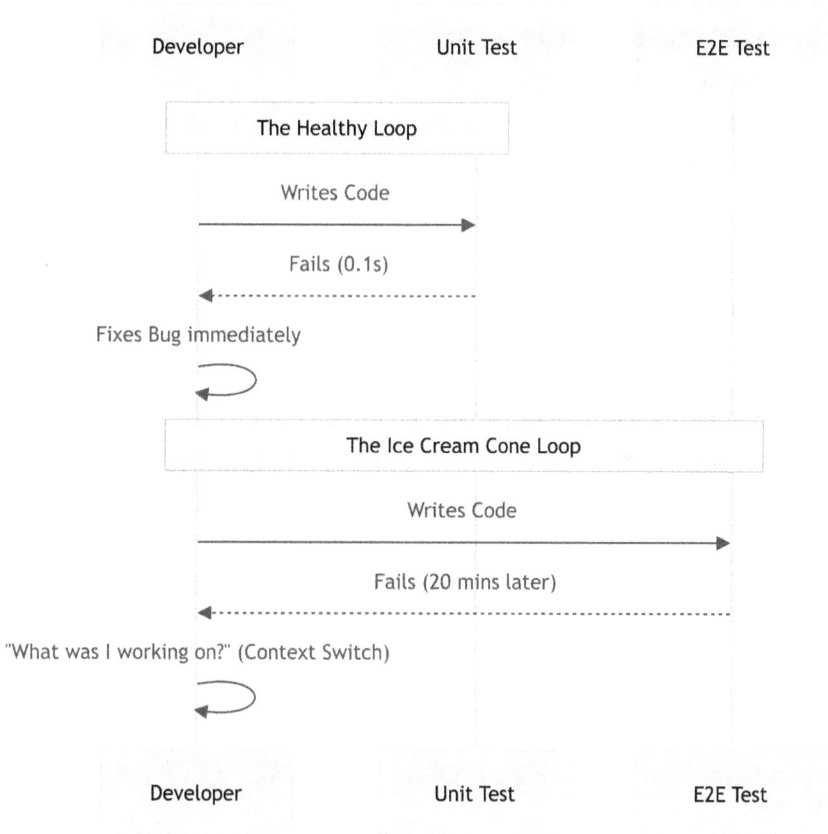

Figure 8.3: Oversized manual/E2E tests slow feedback and amplify context switching

8.9 Conclusion

A healthy Testing Pyramid is about **confidence at the right price**.

- Use **Unit Tests** to verify your logic is sound.
- Use **Integration Tests** to verify your components talk to each other.
- Use **E2E Tests** to verify that the system works for the user.

When you have this safety net in place, you are no longer afraid of your code. You stop coding defensively and start coding creatively. The fear of the "God Class" vanishes, replaced by the confidence that if you break it, you will know immediately.

This confidence is the prerequisite for evolution. With a solid test suite, you can stop merely adding code and start improving it.

Next, we turn that safety into structure. *Chapter 9 (The Discipline of Refactoring)* demonstrates how to utilize this fine code, pay down debt, and maintain a young system safety net to refactor with confidence.

Chapter 9:

The Discipline of Refactoring

Software has a natural tendency to rot.

Physicists call it entropy: the inevitable decline of order into disorder. In software, we call it the "Big Ball of Mud." You start with a clean, elegant design. Then a deadline hits. You add a quick hack. A requirement changes. You copy-paste a function because it's faster than abstracting it. Six months later, you're afraid to touch the billing module because every time you fix a bug there, the login page breaks.

This isn't a failure of skill; it's a failure of maintenance.

Refactoring is the antidote to software entropy. It is not a "cleanup phase" you schedule once a year. It is a continuous, disciplined habit of improving the structure of your code without altering its external behavior. It is the difference between a codebase that ages like wine and one that ages like milk.

Refactoring – changing internal structure without altering externally observable behavior – protects long-term velocity and keeps future changes cheap.

9.1 The Two Hats

Kent Beck, the creator of Extreme Programming, uses a powerful metaphor for development: **The Two Hats**.

When you sit down to code, you are always wearing one of two hats. You must never wear both at the same time.

1. **The Author Hat (Adding Functionality):** You are adding a new feature or fixing a bug. Your goal is to change the behavior of the system. You add new tests and write code to make them pass. You don't worry about code quality yet; you focus on correctness.
2. **The Editor Hat (Refactoring):** You are improving the structure of existing code. You do **not** add any new functionality. You do **not** add new tests (though you might improve existing ones). Your goal is to make the code easier to understand and cheaper to modify.

The golden rule is separation. If you are adding a feature and notice a messy function, you do not fix it while adding the feature. You finish the feature (Author Hat), commit your work, and then switch to the Editor Hat to clean up.

Why? Because trying to do both at once is the fastest way to introduce bugs. When you change structure and behavior simultaneously, and something breaks, you won't know if it was your new logic or your structural change.

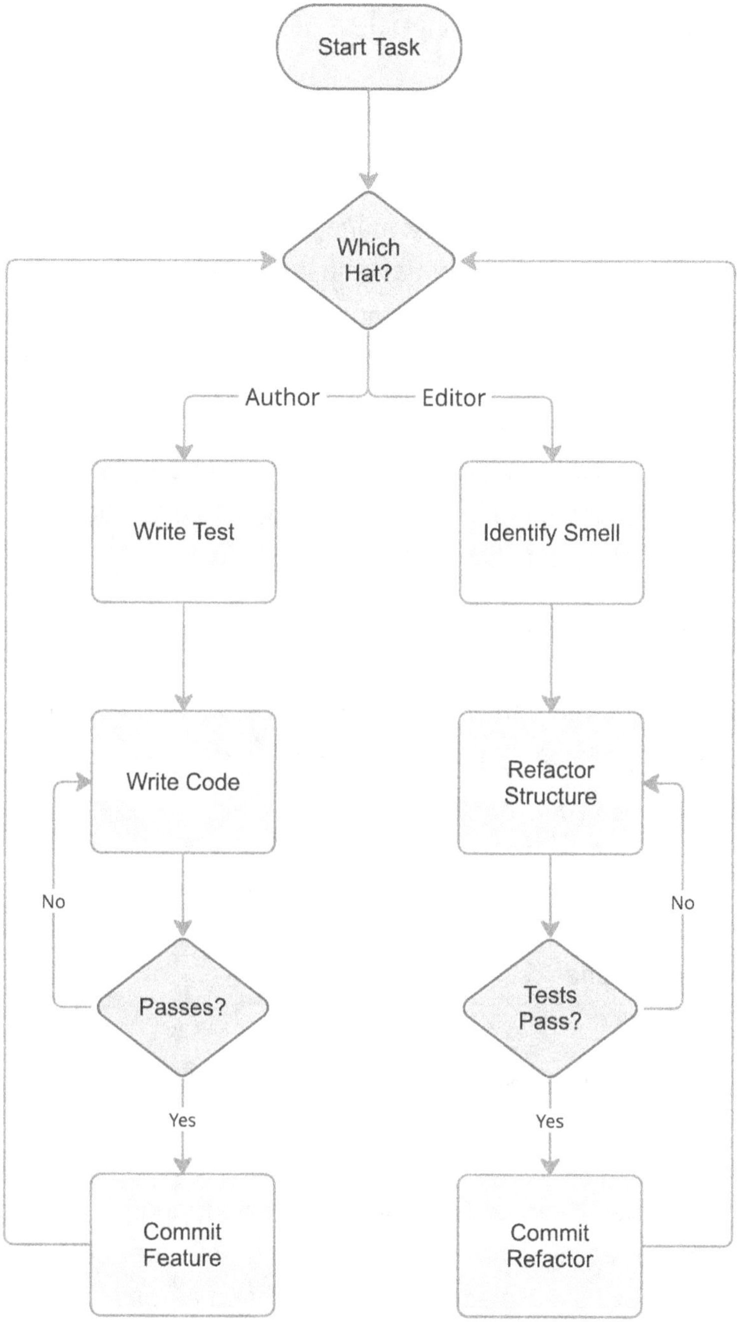

Figure 9.1: The Two Hats – separate adding functionality (Author) from refactoring (Editor) to avoid mixing concerns and reduce defects

9.2 The Boy Scout Rule

The Boy Scouts of America have a simple rule: *"Always leave the campground cleaner than you found it."*

This is an effective strategy for managing technical debt. You don't need to stop development for a month to rewrite the entire system (a dangerous trap known as the "Grand Redesign in the Sky"). Instead, you make small, incremental improvements every time you touch a file.

If you open a file to add a logging statement and notice a variable named `x`, rename it to `retryCount`. If you see a function that's 50 lines long, extract a cohesive block into a helper.

These changes take seconds. But over time, they compound. A team that follows the Boy Scout Rule ends up with a codebase that gets *better* the more they work on it. A team that doesn't ends up with a legacy system that everyone fears.

> **Note**
>
> Refactoring is not about perfection; it's about direction. Is the code slightly better now than it was ten minutes ago? If yes, you're winning.

9.2.1 When to Stop?

Don't scrub the campsite with a toothbrush. Refactoring has diminishing returns. If the code is readable, tested, and you can make your change easily, stop. You are building software, not polishing a museum exhibit. Refactoring is a means to an end, not the end itself.

> ⚠ **Warning**
>
> A full rewrite that promises a "clean slate" often reintroduces the same problems at higher cost. Incremental refactoring preserves proven behavior while improving structure.

9.2.2 Refactoring vs. Rewriting

Refactoring keeps behavior constant while improving structure. Rewriting discards the existing implementation and risks losing hidden domain knowledge, edge-case handling, and battle-tested stability. Favor incremental refactoring unless the architecture is fundamentally misaligned with current requirements.

9.3 The Safety Net

You cannot refactor without tests.

Read that again. **You cannot refactor without tests.**

If you change the structure of code without a comprehensive suite of automated tests to verify that the behavior has not changed, you are not refactoring. You are just changing things and hoping.

Tests are your safety net. They let you move fast. Without them, you move slowly – paralyzed by the fear of breaking something invisible. Before any significant refactoring, ensure the test suite is green. If the code you want to clean up is not tested, your first task is not to refactor but to write a "characterization test" – a test that locks down the current behavior (even the bugs) so you can safely restructure the code.

Your unit, integration, and selective E2E tests from *Chapter 8 (The Testing Pyramid)* form the practical foundation for safe refactoring.

> **Note**
>
> A characterization test records current inputs and outputs so you can preserve externally observable behavior while reshaping internal structure.

9.4 Listening to Your Code

9.4.1 Common Smells and Fixes

Code talks. When structural problems arise, they manifest as "Code Smells." These aren't bugs – the code works – but they are symptoms of decay that suggest deeper design issues.

Just as a fever is a symptom of an infection, a code smell is a symptom of poor design.

Table 9.1: Common code smells with their risks and refactoring strategies

Smell	Description	Risk	Refactoring Move
Duplication	Logic appears in multiple places.	Divergent fixes, defects in missed copy.	Extract Method: Centralize logic and call it.
Long Method	Does too many things (parsing, computing, persisting).	Hidden bugs, low comprehension, slow onboarding.	Extract Method: Split until it reads like a summary.

Smell	Description	Risk	Refactoring Move
Magic Numbers	Unexplained numeric literals (`if status == 4`).	Misuse, misinterpretation of domain meaning.	Replace Magic Number with Constant: Clarify intent.
Primitive Obsession	Overuse of primitives for rich concepts (e.g., phone as string).	Scattered validation, weak invariants.	Introduce Parameter Object / Value Object.

9.4.2 Example: Extract Method & Guard Clauses

Deeply nested `if/else` blocks are hard to read. They force the reader to keep a mental stack of conditions. You can flatten this logic using **guard clauses** (early returns for terminating conditions) and **Extract Method**.

Before: The Arrow of Code

```
# Bad: Deep nesting and mixed responsibilities
def process_order(order):
    if order.is_valid:
        if order.items:
            total = 0
            for item in order.items:
                if item.in_stock:
                    total += item.price

            if total > 0:
```

```
                order.total = total
                order.save()
                return "Success"
            else:
                return "No items in stock"
        else:
            return "Order is empty"
    else:
        return "Invalid order"
```

After: Flat and Readable

```
# Good: Guard clauses and single responsibility
def process_order(order):
    if not order.is_valid:
        return "Invalid order"

    if not order.items:
        return "Order is empty"

    total = _calculate_total(order.items)

    if total == 0:
        return "No items in stock"

    _finalize_order(order, total)
    return "Success"

def _calculate_total(items):
    """Calculates sum of in-stock items."""
    return sum(item.price for item in items if
    ↪  item.in_stock)

def _finalize_order(order, total):
    """Updates and persists the order."""
```

```
    order.total = total
    order.save()
```

Notice how `process_order` now reads like a high-level summary. The details of calculation and persistence are hidden in helpers.

> **Note**
>
> Guard clauses (early returns) reduce cognitive load by eliminating deep nesting and making failure paths explicit.

9.4.3 Example: Meaningful Names

Code is for humans first. If you have to read the implementation to know what a variable holds, the name is a failure.

Before: Cryptic Context

```
// Bad: What is 'd'? What is 86400?
function check(d: number): boolean {
    const n = Date.now();
    return (n - d) < 86400000;
}
```

After: Intent Revealed

```
// Good: The code explains itself
const MILLISECONDS_IN_DAY = 86400000;

function isCreatedWithinLast24Hours(creationTimestamp:
↪   number): boolean {
    const currentTimestamp = Date.now();
    const ageInMilliseconds = currentTimestamp -
     ↪  creationTimestamp;
```

```
    return ageInMilliseconds < MILLISECONDS_IN_DAY;
}
```

9.5 The Cost of Change

Why bother? Why not just write code fast and fix it later?

Because "later" rarely comes, and the cost of change is not linear. In a messy codebase the cost of adding a feature grows exponentially. You spend more time reading code than writing it. You spend more time debugging side effects than delivering value.

Refactoring flattens this curve. It pays the maintenance "tax" upfront to keep the development "rent" low. Unchecked smells steepen the cost-of-change curve; each unrefactored duplication or long method adds cognitive and regression risk.

9.6 Conclusion

Refactoring is not something you ask permission to do. You do not ask your manager, "Can I spend two hours refactoring this module?" any more than a surgeon asks a patient, "Can I spend five minutes washing my hands before I operate?"

It is part of the job. It is the professional standard.

By separating the Author and Editor hats, following the Boy Scout Rule, and listening to code smells, you move from coder (makes things work) to engineer (builds systems that last).

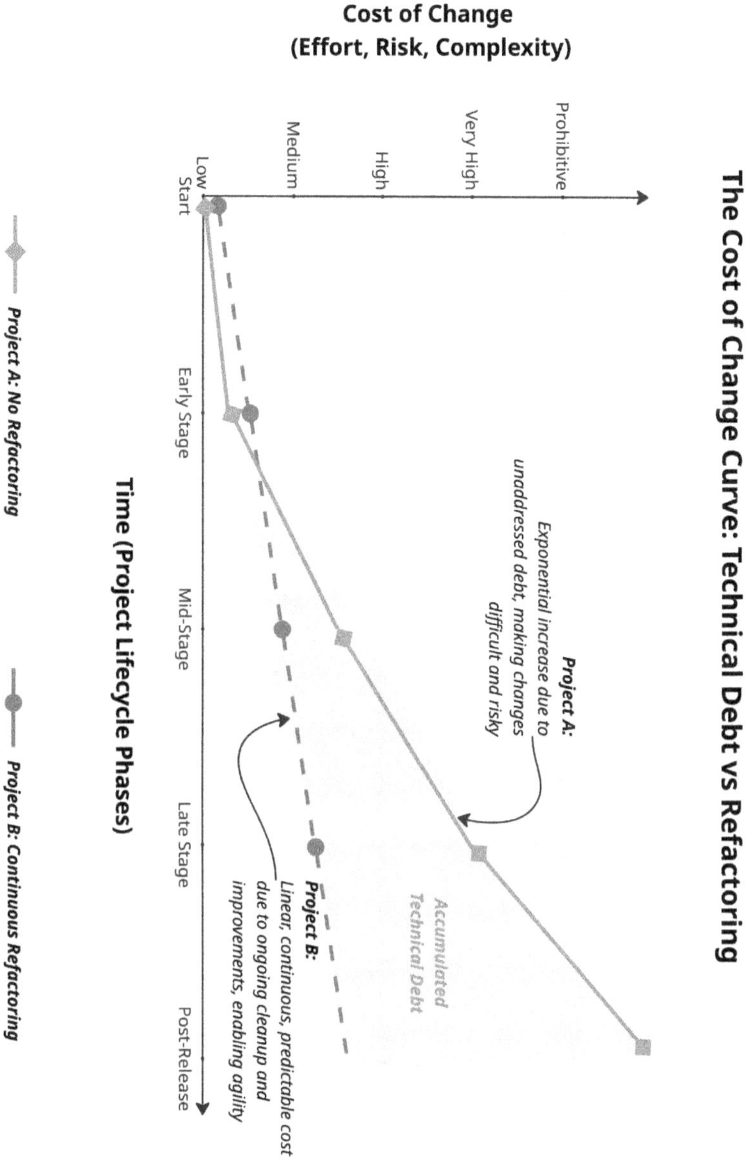

Figure 9.2: Cost of Change: continuous refactoring keeps change cost flatter over time

Next, we look at how to manage these systems at scale. *Chapter 10 (Pillar 1 – Lifecycle Management)* explores how to version, build, and deploy your clean code with confidence.

Part IV

The Core Pillars of Software Engineering

Chapter 10:

Pillar 1 – Lifecycle Management

Software is not a static artifact. It is a living stream of value that flows from your mind, through your keyboard, and into the hands of users.

Many junior engineers view their job as “writing code.” They believe their work is done when the feature works on their laptop. This is a dangerous illusion. The phrase “it works on my machine” is the most expensive sentence in software engineering. It signals that the code relies on a fragile, invisible context – a specific library version, a local database state, or a manual configuration – that does not exist in the real world.

Without disciplined lifecycle practices, teams trade short-term speed for long-term fragility. They suffer from slow incident recovery, unpredictable releases, and silent regressions where fixing one bug creates two more.

Lifecycle Management (often called Application Lifecycle Management or ALM) is the rigorous “factory floor” that transforms raw code into a reliable product. It is the set of disciplines that ensures what works on your machine works for the world, predictably and safely.

10.1 The Source of Truth: Version Control

If your codebase is a story, version control is not just the save button; it is the time machine and the ledger.

In the past, developers often saved files like `script_final.py`, `script_final_v2.py`, and `script_really_final.py`. This is chaos. Modern engineering relies on **Git** as the single source of truth. It records not just *what* changed, but *why* it changed and *who* changed it.

10.1.1 Branching Strategies: Organizing Collaboration

Version control isn't just about history; it's about how teams work together without stepping on each other's toes.

- **Trunk-Based Development**: The modern standard for high-performing teams. Developers merge small, frequent changes directly into the main branch (the "trunk"). This minimizes "merge hell" and encourages continuous integration.
- **GitFlow**: A more rigid model with long-lived feature branches, release branches, and hotfix branches. Useful for packaged software with strict release cycles, but often too slow for web services.

10.1.2 Semantic Versioning: The Contract of Compatibility

How do you know if upgrading a library will break your application? You rely on a contract called **Semantic Versioning** (SemVer). It uses a three-part number format: `MAJOR.MINOR.PATCH` (e.g., `2.14.3`).

- **MAJOR** version when you make incompatible API changes (breaking changes).
- **MINOR** version when you add functionality in a backward-compatible manner.
- **PATCH** version when you make backward-compatible bug fixes.

Respecting this contract allows systems to evolve independently without collapsing.

10.1.3 Beyond Code: Data and Model Versioning

In the age of AI, code is only half the story. If you train a model on a dataset, you must version the data just as strictly as the code. Tools like **DVC (Data Version Control)** or **MLflow** allow you to track which version of a dataset produced which model, ensuring that your experiments are reproducible.

Once history is reliable, we must automate the validation of today's changes. Enter the assembly line.

10.2 The Assembly Line: Continuous Integration (CI)

Imagine building a car by hand. It's romantic, but every car is slightly different, and errors are frequent. Now imagine a robotic assembly line. Every bolt is tightened to the same torque, every time.

Continuous Integration (CI) is the gatekeeper. Every time you push code to the repository, the CI server wakes up. It merges your code with the main branch in an isolated environment and runs a battery of tests.

The Testing Layers

Your CI pipeline should verify the system at multiple levels (recalling the *Chapter 8 (The Testing Pyramid)*):

1. **Unit Tests:** Fast checks for individual logic.
2. **Integration Tests:** Verifying that modules talk to each other correctly.
3. **Contract Tests**: Verifying that a service meets explicit consumer expectations (API shape, fields, error codes) without requiring full end-to-end dependencies.

> **Note**
>
> Contract tests focus on the boundary contract; integration tests exercise real collaborations. They reduce surprise when services evolve.

If the build fails, the line stops. You cannot ship broken code. This feedback loop catches integration errors minutes after they are introduced, rather than weeks later.

10.3 The Artifact: Continuous Delivery (CD)

Continuous Delivery (CD) is the conveyor belt that moves valid code to environments.

10.3.1 The Principle of Immutability

The most critical concept in CD is the **Immutable Artifact**. Once code passes CI, the pipeline packages it into a single binary, Docker container, or zip file.

You build once, and deploy many times. You never rebuild the code for production. You take the same artifact that passed tests in staging and move it to production. This guarantees that the code you tested is the code you run.

> **Note**
>
> **Continuous Delivery** means your code is *always ready* to deploy. **Continuous Deployment** means every change that passes the pipeline is *automatically* deployed to production without human intervention.

10.3.2 Example: The Pipeline Definition

Modern pipelines are defined as code (YAML), living right next to your application source.

```
# .github/workflows/ci-cd.yml
# Intent: Define a standard build-test-publish
↪ pipeline (build once, promote)
name: production-ci

on:
  push:
    branches: [ "main" ]
  pull_request:
    branches: [ "main" ]

permissions:
  contents: read

jobs:
  build-and-test:
    runs-on: ubuntu-latest
```

```yaml
    steps:
      - uses: actions/checkout@v3

      - name: Set up Node.js
        uses: actions/setup-node@v3
        with:
          node-version: '18'
          cache: 'npm'

      - name: Install Dependencies
        run: npm ci

      - name: Run Linter
        run: npm run lint

      - name: Run Unit Tests
        run: npm test

      - name: Build Artifact
        run: npm run build

      - name: Upload Artifact
        uses: actions/upload-artifact@v3
        with:
          name: build-assets
          path: dist/
          retention-days: 7

  # (Optional) A separate deploy job would consume the
↪   uploaded artifact instead of rebuilding.
```

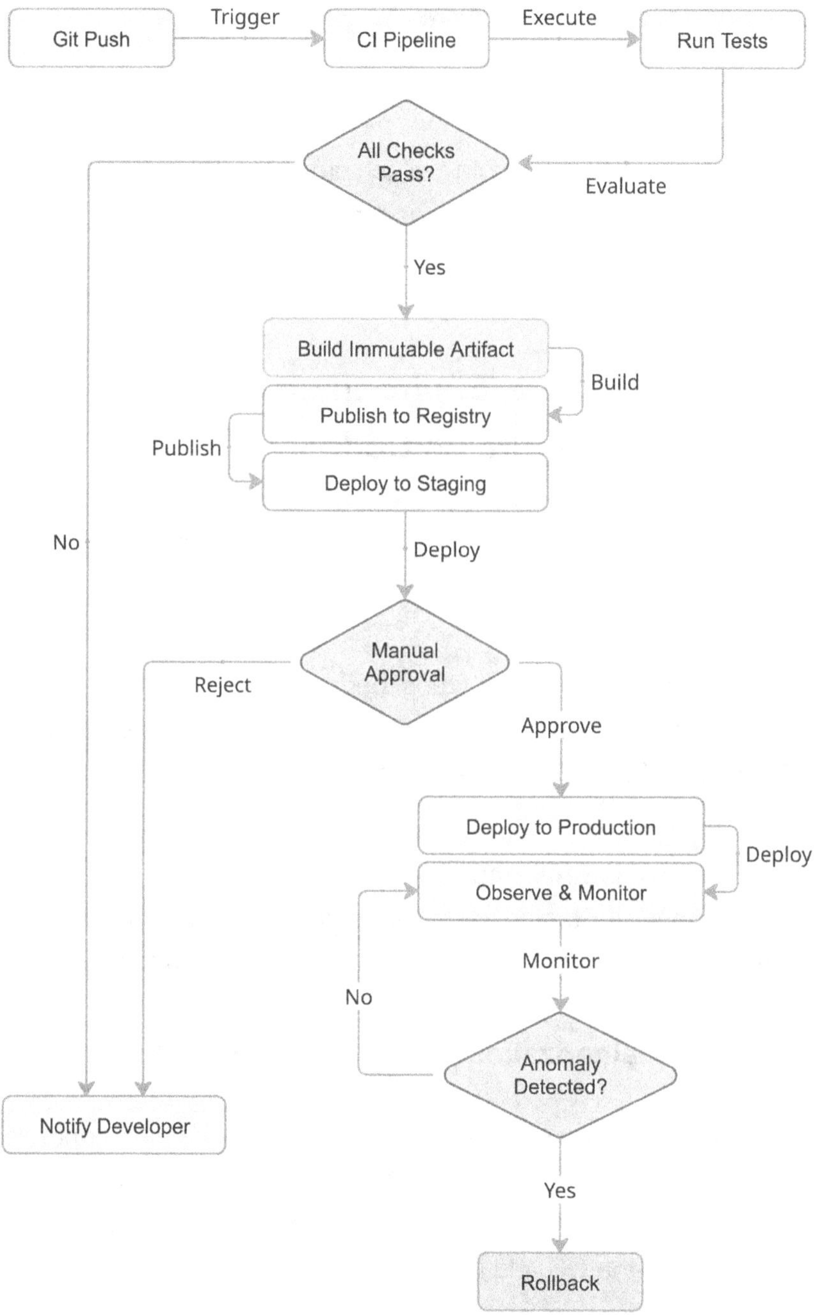

Figure 10.1: CI/CD lifecycle – build once, create immutable artifact, promote the same digest across environments, observe, and roll back fast

10.3.3 Visualizing the Flow

> **Note**
>
> The pipeline builds a single artifact, promotes the exact digest across environments, and uses monitoring plus fast rollback to preserve reliability.

10.4 The Habitat: Environments and Infrastructure as Code

You would never perform a play on opening night without a dress rehearsal. Similarly, software needs different stages:

1. **Development:** Where you experiment (often local).
2. **Staging:** A mirror of production where you test integration.
3. **Production:** Where users live.

The golden rule is **Environment Parity**. Staging must look exactly like Production. If Staging uses a small local database and Production uses a massive cloud cluster, your tests are lying to you.

10.4.1 Containerization: The Shipping Container

To achieve parity, we use containers. Just as a shipping container fits on any ship, truck, or train, a **Docker** container runs the same on your laptop, the CI server, and the production cloud. It bundles your code with the OS and libraries it needs.

```
# Dockerfile
```

```
# Intent: Define a reproducible production runtime
↪ (dependencies pinned via lock file)
FROM node:18.18-alpine AS runtime
WORKDIR /app
COPY package*.json ./
RUN npm ci --only=production # uses package-lock.json
↪ for deterministic install
COPY . .
ENV NODE_ENV=production
# Add non-root user for security hardening
RUN adduser -D app && chown -R app /app
USER app
HEALTHCHECK --interval=30s --timeout=3s --retries=3
↪ CMD node healthcheck.js || exit 1
CMD ["node", "server.js"]
```

10.4.2 Infrastructure as Code (IaC)

To ensure parity, we stop clicking buttons in cloud consoles. We treat **infrastructure as code**. We write code that defines our servers, databases, and networks.

Tools like **Terraform**, **Bicep**, or **Pulumi** allow you to destroy and recreate your entire universe from a text file. This eliminates "**configuration drift**," where a server slowly changes over time until no one knows how it works.

```
# main.tf (Terraform)
# Intent: Define an immutable storage bucket for
↪ application assets (requires AWS creds configured
↪ externally)
provider "aws" {
  region = "us-east-1"
  # Pin provider version for reproducibility
```

```
  # version = "~> 5.0" (add via required_providers
↪  block in terraform stanza for full config)
}

resource "aws_s3_bucket" "app_assets" {
  bucket = "my-app-production-assets"
  tags = {
    Environment = "Production"
    ManagedBy   = "Terraform"
  }
}

resource "aws_s3_bucket_versioning" "versioning" {
  bucket = aws_s3_bucket.app_assets.id
  versioning_configuration {
    status = "Enabled"
  }
}

resource
↪  "aws_s3_bucket_server_side_encryption_configuration"
↪  "encryption" {
  bucket = aws_s3_bucket.app_assets.id
  rule {
    apply_server_side_encryption_by_default {
      sse_algorithm = "AES256"
    }
  }
}

resource "aws_s3_bucket_public_access_block"
↪  "public_block" {
  bucket                  =
↪  aws_s3_bucket.app_assets.id
  block_public_acls       = true
```

```
    block_public_policy     = true
    ignore_public_acls      = true
    restrict_public_buckets = true
}
```

10.4.3 Schema Evolution

Code is easy to change; data is hard. When you change your database schema, you cannot just “deploy” it. You must migrate it. Use the **Expand and Contract** pattern:

1. **Expand:** Add a new column (nullable) to the database.
2. **Migrate:** Deploy code that writes to both old and new columns.
3. **Contract:** Once all data is migrated, remove the old column.

10.5 Orchestration: Deployment Patterns

In the past, deployment was a “Big Bang.” You turned off the old system, installed the new one, and prayed. Modern engineering decouples **Deployment** (moving code to servers) from **Release** (exposing features to users).

10.5.1 Rolling Updates

Imagine resurfacing a highway one lane at a time. Traffic keeps moving in the other lanes. A **Rolling Update** replaces instances of your application one by one. If a new instance fails health checks, the rollout stops, affecting only a tiny fraction of users.

10.5.2 Blue-Green Deployment

You have two identical environments. Blue is live. You deploy to Green. Once Green is healthy, you switch the router to point to Green. If Green fails, you switch back instantly. **Blue-Green Deployment** provides an instant safety net.

10.5.3 Canary Release

You route 1% of traffic to the new version. If no errors occur, you ramp up to 10%, then 50%, then 100%. **Canary Release** limits the "blast radius" of a bad change.

10.6 Progressive Delivery and Control

Deployment gets the code there; progressive delivery controls who sees it.

10.6.1 Feature Flags

The ultimate safety valve is the **Feature Flag**. You deploy code that is "off" by default. You can turn it on for specific users (beta testers) or turn it off instantly if bugs appear, without rolling back the entire deployment.

```
// feature-flags.ts
// Intent: Decouple deployment from release using a
↪  conditional check (runnable stub)

type User = { id: string };

// Stub providers for illustration
```

```
const stripeProvider = { charge: async (_u: User,
↪  amount: number) => amount * 1.0 };
const legacyProvider = { charge: async (_u: User,
↪  amount: number) => amount * 1.0 };

async function getFeatureFlag(flagName: string,
↪  _userId: string): Promise<boolean> {
  // In reality: evaluate remote config / flag service
  return flagName === 'new-stripe-integration';
}

export async function processPayment(user: User,
↪  amount: number) {
  const useNewPaymentProvider = await
  ↪  getFeatureFlag('new-stripe-integration',
  ↪  user.id);
  if (useNewPaymentProvider) {
    // New code path (deployed but controlled)
    const charged = await stripeProvider.charge(user,
    ↪  amount);
    console.log('[payment] stripe', { user: user.id,
    ↪  amount, charged });
    return charged;
  }
  // Old code path (safe fallback)
  const charged = await legacyProvider.charge(user,
  ↪  amount);
  console.log('[payment] legacy', { user: user.id,
  ↪  amount, charged });
  return charged;
}

// Example invocation (not part of production export)
processPayment({ id: 'u1' }, 100).then(r =>
↪  console.log('Result', r));
```

> ⚠ Warning
>
> Retire stale flags. Each long-lived flag adds branching complexity and cognitive load. Treat flag cleanup as a lifecycle task.

10.6.2 Rollback Strategy

Hope is not a strategy. You must have a plan for when things go wrong. A robust rollback relies on the **Detect-Decide-Revert** loop:

1. **Detect:** Monitoring alerts you to a spike in errors.
2. **Decide:** Is this a fix-forward (small bug) or a rollback (critical failure)?
3. **Revert:** Because your artifacts are immutable, you simply redeploy the *previous* artifact. No rebuilding required.

10.7 Change Management and Governance

Lifecycle management is also about accountability.

- **Pull Requests (PRs)**: The primary social mechanism for code quality. A PR is a request for peer review, not just a merge request.
- **Approval Gates**: Critical environments (like Production) often require a manual approval step in the pipeline, ensuring a human has signed off on the release.
- **Auditability:** In regulated industries, you must prove *who* changed *what* and *when*. A good pipeline logs every deployment, linking the running artifact back to the specific Git commit and the person who approved it.

10.8 Lifecycle Starter Checklist

If you want to move from "it works on my machine" to professional engineering, start here:

- ☐ **Version Control:** Are you using a branching strategy (like Trunk-Based)?
- ☐ **CI:** Does every commit trigger an automated build and test run?
- ☐ **Artifacts:** Are you building a single, immutable artifact for all environments?
- ☐ **Parity:** Is your staging environment a true mirror of production?
- ☐ **IaC:** Is your infrastructure defined in code, or are you clicking in the console?
- ☐ **Rollback:** Can you revert to the previous version in under 5 minutes?

10.9 Conclusion

A robust lifecycle is not bureaucracy; it is liberation. When you trust your pipeline to catch errors, your version control to save history, and your deployment strategy to handle rollbacks, you stop fearing the "Deploy" button. You gain the confidence to ship value continuously.

Tools change. Jenkins may be replaced by GitHub Actions; Docker may be replaced by Wasm. But the principles – **automate validation, preserve history, make infrastructure reproducible** – endure.

Now that we have a factory floor that moves code safely, we must ensure the factory itself is secure.

Next, we turn to protection. *Chapter 11 (Pillar 2: Security)* explores how to build trust into every layer of your system, ensuring that your robust pipeline doesn't become a highway for attackers.

Chapter 11:

Pillar 2: Security

Imagine you are building a house. You pour a solid foundation, frame the walls, and install beautiful windows. But you forget to install locks on the doors. You assume that because you are a good neighbor, everyone else is too.

In software, this optimism is dangerous.

Security often feels like the most intimidating pillar for junior engineers. It can seem like a dark art practiced by hackers in hoodies or specialized "Red Teams." You might think, "I'll just build the feature, and the security team will secure it later."

This mindset is a relic of the past. In modern engineering, **security is not a feature you add; it is a quality of the code you write.**

Just as you don't add "correctness" to your code after it's written, you don't add security at the end. Security is the discipline of risk management. It is the practice of empathy for your users, ensuring that the trust they place in your system is never violated.

For this pillar, we treat security as everyday risk management practiced in every function, not a separate review at the end.

11.1 The Security Mindset: Think Like an Adversary

Most engineers are builders. We look at a system and ask, "How do I make this work?" To write secure code, you must also learn to think like a breaker. You must ask, "How could I make this fail?"

Think of a homeowner securing their property. A builder ensures the door opens smoothly. A security-minded homeowner looks at the same door and checks the hinges, the frame strength, and who has a copy of the key. They don't just lock the front door; they consider the back window and the garage.

Zero Trust

The core principle of the security mindset is **Zero Trust**.

In the past, we assumed that anything inside our corporate network (the "intranet") was safe. Today, we assume the network is hostile. We assume that:

1. The network is compromised.
2. The user input is malicious.
3. The third-party library has vulnerabilities.

Never trust. Always verify. Zero Trust extends beyond inputs – it continuously re-evaluates identity, device posture, and context rather than relying on a one-time perimeter decision. Every input that enters your system – whether from a user, a database, or another service – must be treated as a potential threat until validated.

11.2 Defense in Depth

If you visit a medieval castle, you won't find just a single door protecting the king. You will find a moat, a drawbridge, an outer wall, an inner wall, and finally, the keep.

This is **Defense in Depth**.

No single security control is perfect. Firewalls can be bypassed. Passwords can be stolen. Encryption keys can be leaked. If you rely on a single "hard outer shell" to protect your soft, squishy application interior, one crack spells disaster.

Instead, we layer our defenses.

If the attacker bypasses the firewall (the moat), they still face authentication (the drawbridge). If they steal a password, they still need permissions (the guards). If they get to the database, the data is encrypted (the vault). Protect data in transit too – use TLS or mTLS between every hop.

Even if you don't run firewalls or gateways, your code is one of those layers. Input validation, authorization checks, and safe defaults are the inner walls you control. Add one more layer: monitored audit logs. Silent failures become breaches; visible anomalies become incidents you can contain. A WAF cannot stop malicious authenticated traffic; explicit AuthZ policy checks and least-privilege data access are essential.

11.3 The Principle of Least Privilege

Imagine checking into a hotel. The receptionist gives you a key card. That card opens your room and the gym. It does not open the room next door, the manager's office, or the safe behind the counter.

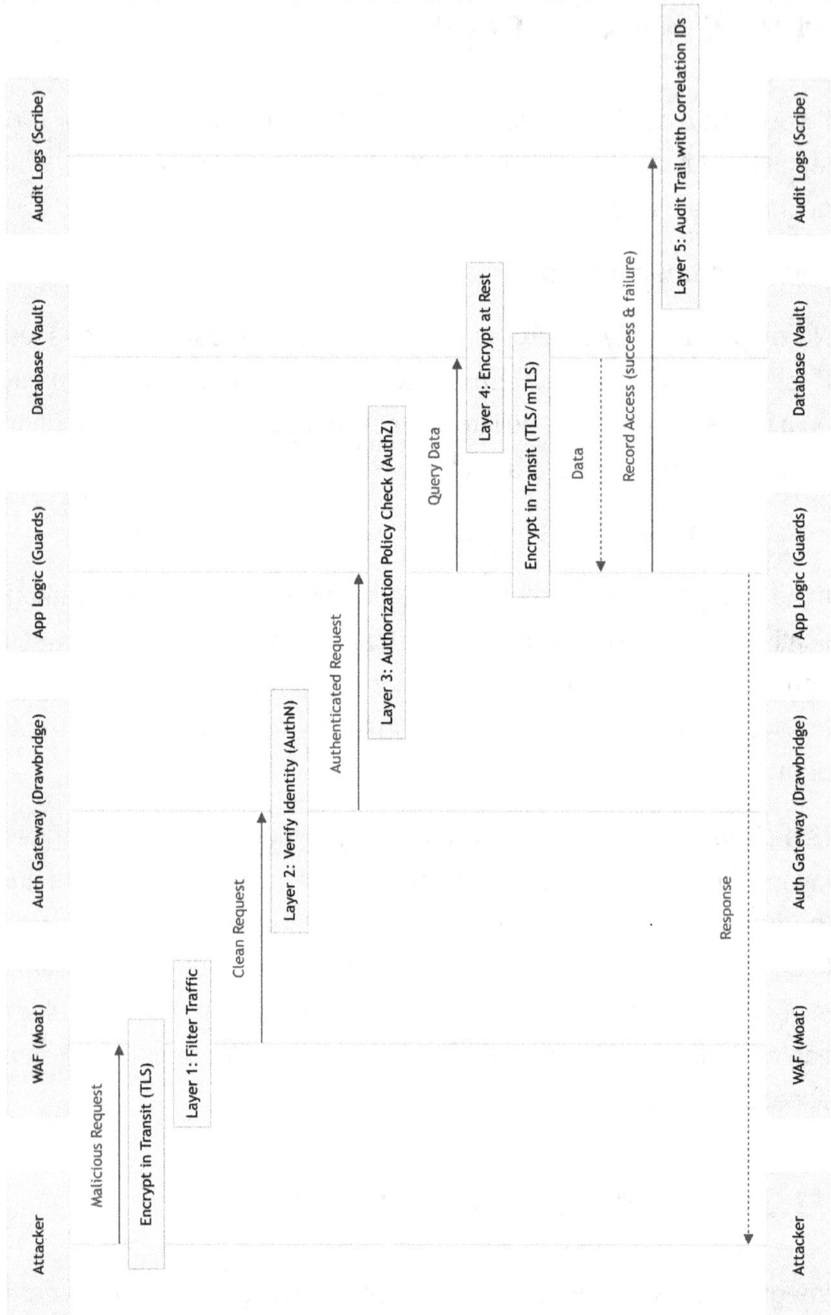

Figure 11.1: Defense in Depth – layered controls: perimeter, authentication, authorization, encryption, and monitored audit logs

This is the **Principle of Least Privilege**.

Every user, service, and process should have only the **minimum permissions necessary** to perform its function.

If your web application only needs to *read* user profiles, the database user it connects with should not have `DROP TABLE` permissions. If a hacker compromises that application, the damage they can do is limited. We call this limiting the **blast radius**.

Example: Broken Access Control (IDOR)

A common violation of this principle is Insecure Direct Object References (IDOR). This is a classic example of **Broken Access Control**, consistently ranked #1 in the OWASP Top 10 vulnerabilities. It occurs when an application provides direct access to objects based on user-supplied input without checking permissions.

Here is a vulnerable endpoint in Python using FastAPI:

```
# ⊗ Bad: Trusting the user input blindly
@app.get("/receipts/{receipt_id}")
def get_receipt(receipt_id: int):
    # The code fetches the receipt just because the ID
    ↪ exists.
    # Any user can change the ID in the URL to see
    ↪ anyone's receipt.
    # Also risks exposing internal fields like
    ↪ 'created_by_user_id' or 'internal_cost'.
    receipt = database.fetch_receipt(receipt_id)
    return receipt
```

And here is the secure version that enforces privilege and sanitizes the response:

```
from fastapi import Depends, HTTPException
from pydantic import BaseModel
from datetime import datetime
from decimal import Decimal

# Define a safe response schema to avoid leaking
↪   internal fields
class ReceiptOut(BaseModel):
    id: int
    total: Decimal
    issued_at: datetime

# ✅ Good: Verifying ownership and filtering output
@app.get("/receipts/{receipt_id}",
↪   response_model=ReceiptOut)
def get_receipt(receipt_id: int, current_user: User =
↪   Depends(get_current_user)):
    receipt = database.fetch_receipt(receipt_id)

    # Check if the receipt belongs to the user
    ↪   requesting it
    if receipt.owner_id != current_user.id:
        # Return 403 Forbidden (or 404 to hide
        ↪   existence)
        raise HTTPException(status_code=403,
        ↪   detail="Not authorized")

    return receipt
```

> **Note**
>
> Prefer consistent error semantics (403 vs 404) and log attempted access with context (user ID, resource ID, correlation ID) for investigation. Use `async def` endpoints when your stack supports it; imports and scaffolding are omitted here for brevity.

In the second example, we don't just ask "Does this receipt exist?" We ask, "Does this user have the privilege to see this receipt?" We also ensure we only return the data we intend to share.

11.4 Secure by Design

Modern cars come with seatbelts, airbags, and crumple zones standard. You don't buy a car and then pay extra to install the brakes. Safety is built into the design.

Secure by Design means considering security requirements before you write a single line of code. It means making the secure path the easiest path. This directly aligns with the OWASP Top 10 category "Insecure Design."

11.4.1 Threat Modeling

You don't need to be a security expert to do basic threat modeling. You just need to ask four questions during your design phase:

1. **What are we building?** (Diagram the data flow)
2. **What could go wrong?** (Identify threats using a framework like STRIDE)
3. **What are we going to do about it?** (Plan mitigations)

4. **Did we do a good job?** (Validate)

The **STRIDE** model helps you categorize threats systematically:

- **S**poofing: Pretending to be someone else.
- **T**ampering: Modifying data or code.
- **R**epudiation: Denying an action took place (lack of logging).
- **I**nformation Disclosure: Exposing sensitive data.
- **D**enial of Service: Crashing or slowing down the system.
- **E**levation of Privilege: Gaining unauthorized capabilities.

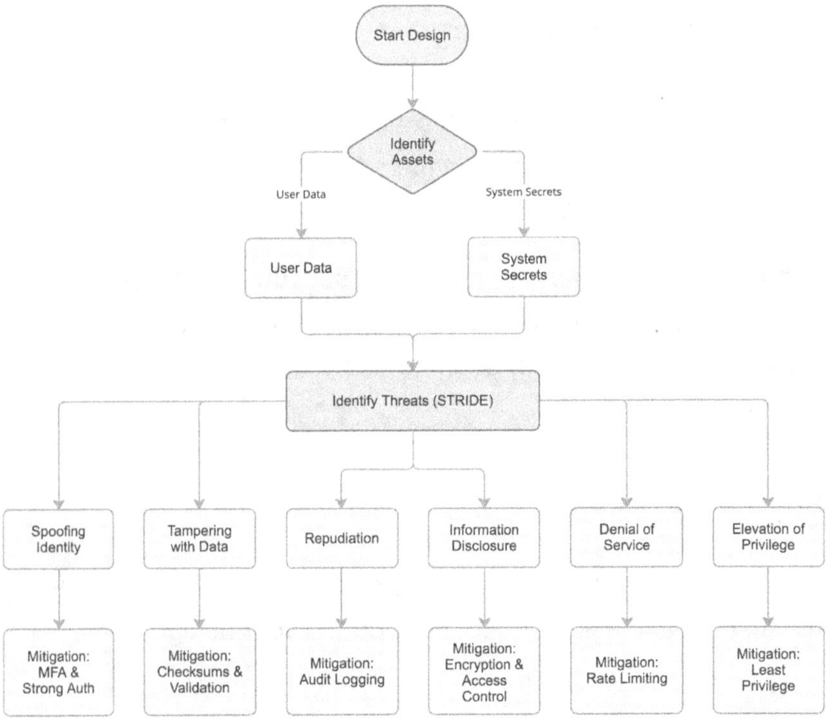

Figure 11.2: STRIDE threat modeling – map threats (Spoofing, Tampering, Repudiation, Information Disclosure, Denial of Service, Elevation of Privilege) to concrete mitigations

Mitigation examples (expand as needed):

- Spoofing: MFA, signed tokens, mTLS.
- Tampering: HMACs, code signing, integrity checks.
- Repudiation: immutable/tamper-evident logs, time-stamps.
- Information Disclosure: encryption, masking, data minimization, access reviews.
- Denial of Service: rate limiting, timeouts, backpressure, circuit breakers.
- Elevation of Privilege: least privilege, sandboxing/isolation, privilege separation.

11.4.2 Example: Sanitizing Output

One of the simplest threats revealed by even a basic threat modeling exercise is: “What if untrusted user content runs as code in the browser?” That is Cross-Site Scripting (XSS).

Another common design flaw is trusting data when displaying it. If you allow users to submit a “Bio” for their profile, and you render that bio directly to the screen, a malicious user could submit a JavaScript script instead of text.

To prevent this, we must distinguish between **encoding** (converting special characters to safe HTML entities) and **sanitizing** (removing unsafe tags while keeping safe ones).

In TypeScript (React), we must ensure data is treated as content, not code.

```
// ❌ Bad: Rendering raw HTML from user input
// If user.bio is "<img src=x onerror=alert(1)>", the
↪ script runs.
<div dangerouslySetInnerHTML={{ __html: user.bio }} />
```

```
// ✅ Good: Using default data binding (Output
↪ Encoding)
// React automatically escapes this, rendering the
↪ script as harmless text.
<div>{user.bio}</div>

// ✅ Good: Explicit sanitization if HTML is truly
↪ needed
// Use a library like DOMPurify to strip dangerous
↪ tags but keep formatting (e.g., <b>, <i>).
import DOMPurify from 'dompurify';

const cleanBio = DOMPurify.sanitize(user.bio);
<div dangerouslySetInnerHTML={{ __html: cleanBio }} />
```

> **Note**
>
> Consider a restrictive Content Security Policy (CSP) to reduce XSS impact, and avoid placing user content in attributes or the `style` prop without strict validation.

Threat modeling helps you find risks specific to your design, but you don't have to discover common vulnerabilities from scratch.

11.5 Industry Standards: The Map of the Territory

You do not need to discover every vulnerability the hard way. The security industry has already mapped the minefield for you.

While principles like Zero Trust guide your mindset, industry standards provide a concrete checklist of "what not to do."

11.5.1 OWASP Top 10

The **Open Web Application Security Project (OWASP)** publishes a list of the ten most critical web application security risks. It is the industry standard for awareness.

- **What it is:** A broad consensus on the most critical security risks to web applications.
- **How to use it:** Read it once a year. Ensure you understand what "Injection," "Broken Access Control," and "Cryptographic Failures" actually mean.
- **ASVS Levels:** Use OWASP ASVS as a verification baseline (L1 for all apps, L2 for sensitive data, L3 for high assurance systems).

11.5.2 CWE/SANS Top 25

While OWASP focuses on high-level risks, the **Common Weakness Enumeration (CWE)** Top 25 lists the most dangerous software errors.

- **What it is:** A list of specific coding errors (like buffer overflows or null pointer dereferences) that lead to vulnerabilities.
- **How to use it:** Use it to configure your static analysis tools (linters) to catch these specific patterns automatically.
- **Practice:** Map static analysis findings to CWE IDs for consistent reporting.

11.5.3 Other Essential Frameworks

- **NIST SSDF (Secure Software Development Framework):** A set of fundamental, sound, and secure software development practices.

- **CIS Benchmarks:** Best practices for securely configuring systems (e.g., hardening your cloud servers or containers).
- **Software Composition Analysis (SCA):** Automate dependency vulnerability checks (e.g., Dependabot/Renovate) and review advisories.
- **SBOMs:** Produce a Software Bill of Materials (SPDX/CycloneDX) to track dependencies across builds.
- **Secrets Management:** Use a vault/KMS (e.g., AWS Secrets Manager, Azure Key Vault, Google Secret Manager, or HashiCorp Vault). Never hardcode secrets; rotate regularly.

> **Further Reading**
>
> Visit https://owasp.org to explore the Top 10 and the **ASVS (Application Security Verification Standard)** for a comprehensive testing checklist.

11.6 Conclusion

Security is not about saying "no." It is about saying "yes, safely."

As an engineer, you are the guardian of your user's data. Every time you validate an input, check a permission, or encrypt a sensitive field, you are honoring that trust. You don't need to be a security expert to write secure code; you just need to be a thoughtful one.

Three Daily Habits for Secure Code:

1. **Validate Inputs:** Never trust data entering your function.
2. **Check Permissions:** Just because a user *can* request data doesn't mean they *should* see it.
3. **Escape Outputs:** Treat all user content as potentially hostile code.

4. **Scan Dependencies:** Regularly check your libraries for known vulnerabilities.

Next, we turn the lights on. *Chapter 12 (Pillar 3 Observability – Building Systems You Can See and Understand)* explores how to make your system's internal state visible, so you can detect and diagnose issues before your users do.

Chapter 12:

Pillar 3 Observability – Building Systems You Can See and Understand

It's 2:00 AM. Your phone buzzes on the nightstand. A notification from the alerting system reads: "High Latency: API Gateway."

You open your laptop, squinting at the screen. You SSH into a server and run `top`. CPU is fine. Memory is fine. You check the database logs; they look normal. Yet, customer support tickets are piling up – users say the app is "stuck." You stare at a black box. You know *something* is wrong, but you have no idea *what*, *where*, or *why*.

This feeling of helplessness is the absence of observability.

Early in your career, you might debug by staring at code or adding `print("here")` statements. That works when the code runs on your machine. It fails catastrophically when your code runs across fifty containers, three cloud regions, and relies on a non-deterministic AI model.

Observability is a measure of how well you can understand a system's internal state purely by inspecting its external outputs. It is the difference between guessing and knowing. It turns the lights on in the dark room of distributed systems.

12.1 The Cockpit: Signals and Semantic Instrumentation

Imagine an air traffic controller trying to manage a busy airport by looking out the window with binoculars. They might see a plane landing, but they don't know its flight number, fuel level, or destination. They operate on visuals alone.

Now, imagine the radar screen. Each blip has a transponder code, altitude, and speed. The controller doesn't need to see the metal bird to understand its behavior. They have *instrumentation*.

In software, we rely on three primary signals – the "Three Pillars of Observability" – to build our radar screen: Logs, Metrics, and Traces.

12.1.1 Logs: The Narrative of Events

Logs are discrete records of events. They answer the question: *"What happened?"*

- A bad log shouts into the void: `Error: failed.`
- A good log is a chapter in a story: `[2025-10-12 14:00:01] [ERROR] [PaymentService] [UserID: 12345] Payment gateway timeout after 5000ms.`

The most critical shift is from **unstructured text** to **structured logging**. Text logs are for humans to read one by one; structured logs (JSON) are for machines to aggregate and query.

> **Note**
>
> Always include a "Correlation ID" (or Request ID) in your logs. This unique string ties together every log entry generated by a single user request across multiple services.

> **Warning**
>
> Sanitize your logs. Never log PII (Personally Identifiable Information) like passwords, credit card numbers, or raw user data. Use hashing or tokenization if you need to track specific users. Ensure your log retention policies comply with regulations (e.g., GDPR) and delete logs automatically after a set period (e.g., 30 days).

Example: Structured Logging in TypeScript

This Express.js middleware ensures every request gets a unique ID, and every log entry includes it.

```
// middleware/logger.ts
import { Request, Response, NextFunction } from
↪  'express';
import { v4 as uuidv4 } from 'uuid';

// Define a structured log format
interface LogEntry {
  timestamp: string;
  level: 'INFO' | 'ERROR' | 'WARN';
  correlationId: string;
  message: string;
  context?: Record<string, any>;
}
```

```
// Middleware to attach a correlation ID to the
↪ request
export const correlationMiddleware = (req: Request,
↪ res: Response, next: NextFunction) => {
  // Prefer W3C Trace Context headers if available,
  ↪ else generate new ID
  const correlationId = req.headers['traceparent'] as
  ↪ string || req.headers['x-correlation-id'] as
  ↪ string || uuidv4();
  // Attach to request object for use in downstream
  ↪ handlers
  (req as any).correlationId = correlationId;
  // Return it to the client for debugging
  res.setHeader('x-correlation-id', correlationId);
  next();
};

// Helper function to emit structured logs
export const logInfo = (req: Request, message: string,
↪ context = {}) => {
  const entry: LogEntry = {
    timestamp: new Date().toISOString(),
    level: 'INFO',
    correlationId: (req as any).correlationId,
    message,
    context,
  };
  // In production, pipe to stdout for collector
  ↪ ingestion (e.g., Fluentd)
  console.log(JSON.stringify(entry));
};

export const logError = (req: Request, message:
↪ string, error: Error) => {
  const entry: LogEntry = {
```

```
    timestamp: new Date().toISOString(),
    level: 'ERROR',
    correlationId: (req as any).correlationId,
    message,
    context: {
      stack: error.stack,
      name: error.name
    },
  };
  console.error(JSON.stringify(entry));
};
```

12.1.2 Metrics: The Pulse of the System

If logs are a diary, metrics are vital signs. They answer the question: *"Is it happening a lot?"*

Metrics are numerical data measured over time. They are cheap to store and fast to query. You use them to spot trends.

- **Counters:** "Total requests: 10,500"
- **Gauges:** "Current memory usage: 512MB"
- **Histograms:** "99% of requests finished in under 200ms" (Prefer histograms for latency to calculate percentiles like p95/p99).

The Golden Signals. Google's SRE book defines four key metrics you should monitor for every user-facing system:

- **Latency:** Time it takes to serve a request.
- **Traffic:** Demand placed on your system (e.g., req/sec).
- **Errors:** Rate of requests that fail.

- **Saturation:** How "full" your service is (e.g., CPU, memory, I/O).

Don't alert on logs – they are too slow and noisy. Alert on metrics. When the "Error Rate" metric spikes above 1%, you wake up. Then, you look at the logs to see *why*.

12.1.3 Traces: The Map of Causality

In a distributed system, a single user click might trigger calls to the Auth Service, the Database, the Payment Gateway, and an AI Model. If the user waits 5 seconds, which service is to blame?

Tracing answers the question: *"Where did the time go?"*

As systems grow, they fragment. A monolith becomes microservices; a database becomes a data lake. In this fragmented world, causality is lost. Distributed tracing restores this causality by stitching events together using a **Trace ID** that propagates across network boundaries.

A **Trace** represents the entire journey of a request. It consists of **Spans**, which represent individual units of work (e.g., "Query Database", "Call OpenAI API").

In the Figure 12.1 and Figure 12.2, if the total latency spikes to 2 seconds, the trace visualization will show you exactly which bar is longer. Is it the Database query? Or is the Model Service hanging? You stop guessing and start fixing.

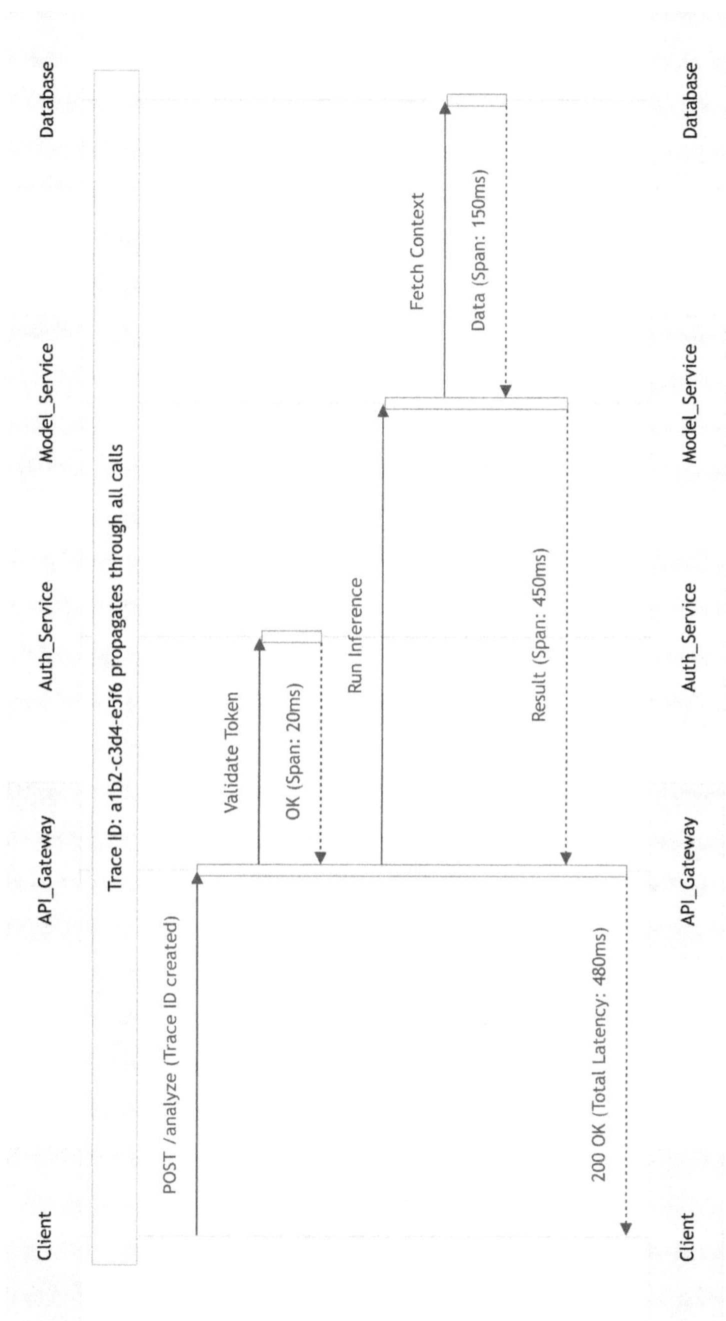

Figure 12.1: Distributed trace timeline – spans across services (Auth, DB, Payment, Model) reveals sequence of service calls

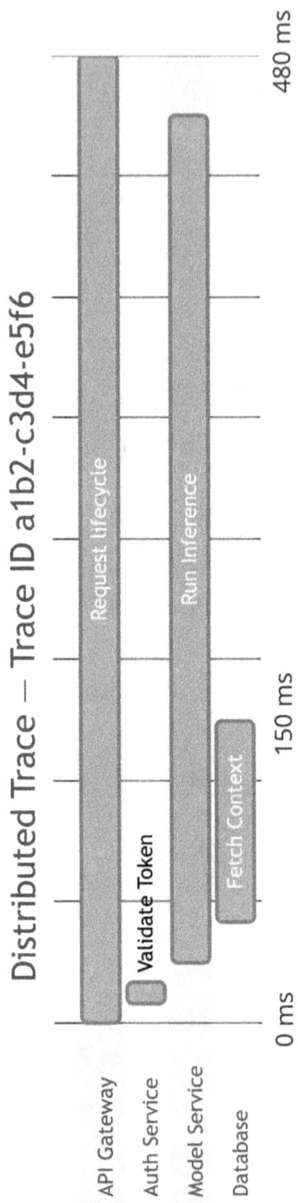

Figure 12.2: Distributed trace timeline – spans across services (Auth, DB, Payment, Model) reveal where latency accumulates

Example: OpenTelemetry Tracing in Python

This example uses the OpenTelemetry library to create a span for a specific operation, adding context that helps debugging later.

```
# services/pricing_service.py
from opentelemetry import trace
from opentelemetry.trace import Status, StatusCode
import time

tracer = trace.get_tracer(__name__)

def calculate_price(item_id: str, user_tier: str) ->
↪   float:
    # Start a new span as a child of the current
    ↪   context
    # Note: Requires OpenTelemetry SDK and Exporter
    ↪   (e.g., OTLP over gRPC/HTTP) setup in app
    ↪   initialization
    with
    ↪   tracer.start_as_current_span("calculate_price")
    ↪   as span:
        # Add attributes (metadata) to the span
        span.set_attribute("item.id", item_id)
        span.set_attribute("user.tier", user_tier)
        # AI-specific attributes for reproducibility
        span.set_attribute("model.id", "gpt-4-turbo")
        span.set_attribute("temperature", 0.2)
        span.set_attribute("dataset.version",
↪   "v2025.10.01")

        try:
            # Simulate work
            time.sleep(0.1)

            if user_tier == "premium":
```

```
            return 0.0  # Free for premium

        return 9.99

    except Exception as e:
        # Record the error in the trace
        span.record_exception(e)
        span.set_status(Status(StatusCode.ERROR))
        raise
```

12.2 From Metrics to Meaning: SLIs and SLOs

Collecting data is easy; deciding what matters is hard.

Imagine going to a doctor.

- **Doctor:** "How are you?"
- **You:** "My white blood cell count is 4,500 per microliter."
- **Doctor:** "Okay… but do you feel sick?"

Engineers often obsess over "white blood cell counts" (CPU usage, disk I/O) rather than "feeling sick" (Can the user load the page?).

To fix this, we use a hierarchy of reliability targets:

1. **SLI (Service Level Indicator):** The measurement. *What are we measuring?*
    - *Example:* The percentage of HTTP requests that return a 200 OK status code within 300ms.
2. **SLO (Service Level Objective):** The target. *What is "good enough"?*

- *Example:* 99.9% of requests must meet the SLI over a 30-day window.

3. **SLA (Service Level Agreement):** The promise. *What happens if we fail?*

   - *Example:* If we drop below 99.0%, we refund the customer 10% of their bill.

> ⚠ Warning
>
> Never alert on SLAs. Alert on SLOs. You want to be woken up *before* you owe the customer money, not after.

> Note
>
> For the economics behind choosing availability targets ("the cost of nines") and how error budgets balance velocity with stability, see *Chapter 14 (Pillar 5 – Reliability and Resilience)*.

12.3 The Error Budget

The gap between 100% perfection and your SLO (e.g., `100% - 99.9% = 0.1%`) is your **Error Budget**.

This concept is powerful. It acknowledges that failure is inevitable. As long as you have error budget remaining, you can push code faster, run experiments, and take risks. If you burn through your budget, you freeze deployments and focus on stability.

Example: Evaluating an SLO

This snippet calculates whether a service is meeting its availability SLO based on a rolling window of results.

```
// Observability/SloMonitor.cs
using System;
using System.Collections.Generic;
using System.Linq;

public class SloMonitor
{
    private readonly Queue<bool> _requestResults = new
    ↪  Queue<bool>();
    private const int WindowSize = 1000; // Size based
    ↪  on traffic volume (e.g., 10 mins of traffic)
    private const double TargetAvailability = 0.99; //
    ↪  99% SLO

    public void RecordRequest(bool isSuccess)
    {
        if (_requestResults.Count >= WindowSize)
        {
            _requestResults.Dequeue();
        }
        _requestResults.Enqueue(isSuccess);
    }

    public bool IsSloBreached()
    {
        if (_requestResults.Count < WindowSize) return
        ↪  false; // Not enough data

        int successCount = _requestResults.Count(r =>
        ↪  r);
```

```
        double currentAvailability =
        ↪ (double)successCount /
        ↪ _requestResults.Count;

        // In a real system, alert only if breach is
        ↪ sustained (e.g., for N consecutive checks)
        return currentAvailability <
        ↪ TargetAvailability;
    }
}
```

With our targets defined, we now turn these measurements into continuous visibility and actionable alerts.

12.4 Monitoring: From Panels to Signals

Dashboards are for looking. Monitoring is for knowing. A common mistake is building "wall of graphs" dashboards that look impressive but hide problems.

Focus your monitoring on:

- **Golden Signals:** (Latency, Traffic, Errors, Saturation) on the main dashboard.
- **Synthetic Probes:** Robots that simulate user journeys (e.g., "Login -> Search -> Checkout") every minute to verify uptime from the outside in.
- **Cost & Drift:** For AI systems, monitor token usage costs and "model drift" (is the model's accuracy degrading over time?).

> **Further Reading**
>
> Synthetic probes complement – but do not replace – E2E tests in CI. See *Chapter 8 (The Testing Pyramid)* for how to structure tests for fast, reliable feedback.

12.5 Alerting: From Noise to Action

Alerts must be urgent, actionable, and rare. If your phone buzzes, it should mean a human *must* take action now.

- **Alert on Symptoms, not Causes:** Alert when "Checkout Failed," not when "CPU is high." High CPU might be fine; failed checkouts are never fine.
- **Eliminate Noise:** Use multi-window alerts (e.g., "Error rate > 1% for 5 minutes"). Single spikes happen; sustained failures matter.
- **Severity Tiers:** Page on-call engineers only for user-impacting outages (Sev-1). Route warnings (Sev-2/3) to a ticket queue or chat channel for next-day review.
- **Escalation Policies:** If the on-call engineer doesn't acknowledge in 15 minutes, page the backup. If they don't answer, page the manager.
- **Maintenance Windows:** Configure your alerting system to auto-silence during planned maintenance to avoid "crying wolf."

> **Note**
>
> After triage, common mitigations include resilience patterns (rate limiting, circuit breakers, timeouts, retries) from *Chapter 14 (Pillar 5 – Reliability and Resilience)*.

12.6 Observability in the AI Era

AI introduces a new layer of opacity. A traditional function `add(2, 2)` always returns 4. An LLM prompt `summarize this` might return a perfect paragraph today and a hallucination tomorrow.

Observability for AI systems demands new signals:

1. **Input/Output Logging:** You must log the prompt and the completion (sanitized for PII) to understand model behavior.
2. **Token Usage & Cost:** Metrics for token counts are essential for financial observability. Monitor cost per request and p95 token usage.
3. **Model Versioning:** Traces must include attributes like `model_id`, `dataset_version`, and `temperature`. You cannot debug a regression if you don't know which model version served the request.
4. **Feedback Loops:** Did the user accept the suggestion? This "thumbs up/down" signal (acceptance rate) is the ultimate SLI for AI quality. Define acceptance clearly (e.g., "user did not override within 5 minutes").

12.7 Lineage: Data $\rightarrow$ Model $\rightarrow$ Behavior

In traditional software, code determines behavior. In AI systems, data determines behavior. If your model starts hallucinating, you need to know not just *what* code is running, but *what* data it was trained on.

Data Lineage tracks the flow of data from source to model. **Model Lineage** links a specific inference back to the training dataset, hyperparameters, and code version.

Your observability pipeline must link these artifacts. When a trace shows a failure, you should be able to click through to the specific model version and the dataset hash it used.

12.8 Designing an Observability Architecture

You don't just "install" observability. You design it like a data pipeline.

1. **Instrumentation:** The code emits signals (SDKs).
2. **Collection:** An agent (like the OpenTelemetry Collector) gathers, batches, and filters the data.
3. **Storage:** Specialized databases store the data (e.g., Prometheus for metrics, Elasticsearch/Loki for logs, Jaeger/Tempo for traces).
4. **Visualization:** Dashboards (Grafana) allow humans to explore the data.

> **Further Reading**
>
> Explore the **OpenTelemetry** project. It is the industry standard for generating and collecting telemetry data in a vendor-neutral way.

12.9 Conclusion

Observability isn't a tool you buy. It's a culture you build. It requires you to care about what happens to your code after it leaves your machine.

When you build observable systems, you stop fearing production. You replace the panic of the 2:00 AM pager call with the calm confi-

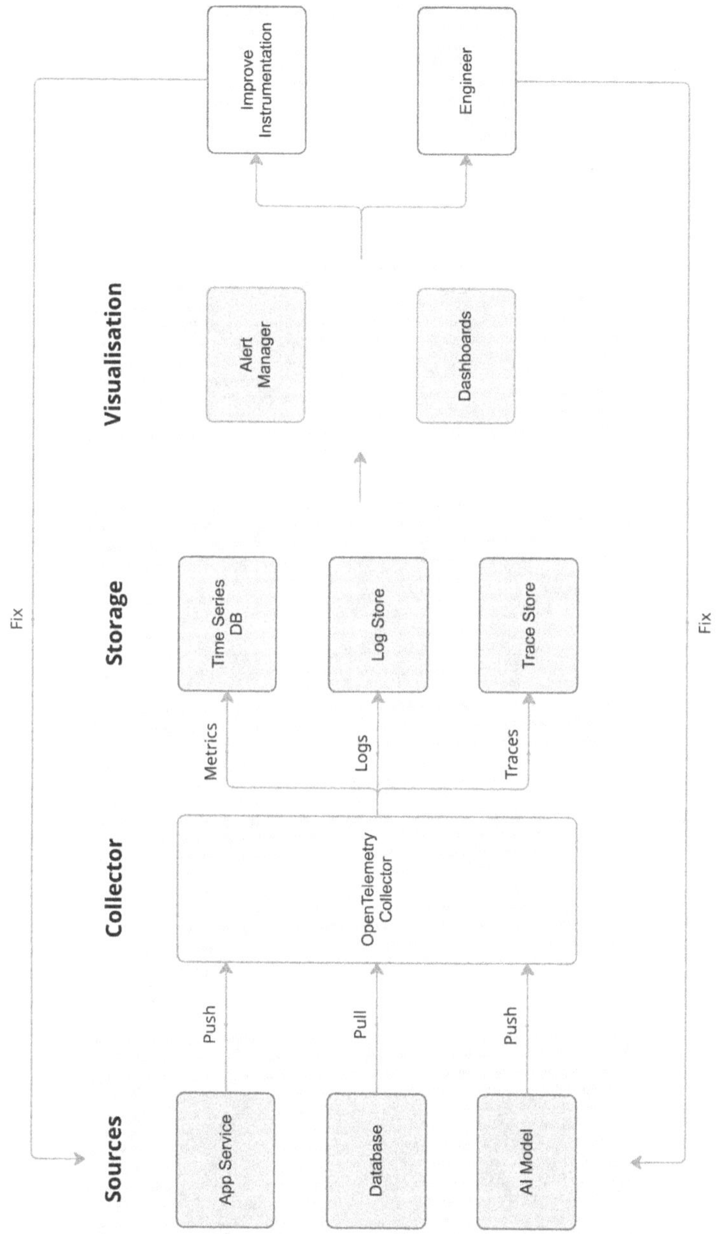

Figure 12.3: Observability architecture – instrument, collect via OpenTelemetry, store (metrics/logs/traces), visualize and alert for action

dence of a detective who has all the clues. You move from "I think it's broken" to "I know why it's slow, and here is the fix."

Next, we will look at how to structure your code so that it is easy to navigate and change. *Chapter 13 (Pillar 4 – Architecture and Design)* explores how to organize complexity before it overwhelms you.

Part V

Advanced Pillars of System Design

Chapter 13:

Pillar 4 – Architecture and Design

Architecture is often misunderstood. Junior engineers may treat it as a mystical activity performed by "Senior Architects" in ivory towers – people who draw boxes on whiteboards and hand down immutable laws – or confuse it with folder layout, arguing about where to put a helper file.

In reality, architecture is not about drawing static diagrams; it is the continuous process of making decisions that are hard to change later.

If code is bricks and mortar, architecture is zoning law and the foundation. You can repaint a wall (design), but you cannot easily move plumbing or rezone residential into industrial (architecture).

This chapter will help you see your code through the lens of a system architect. You will learn to control complexity, manage trade-offs, and build systems that can evolve without collapsing under their own weight.

13.1 Architecture vs Design

Architecture sets the system's shape; design fills it in. Think city planning versus interior design: you can move a couch, but rezoning the neighborhood is hard.

Use reversibility to tell them apart. Architectural choices are hard-to-reverse one-way doors (data model, public APIs, deployment topology). Design choices are two-way doors (class names, private refactors) you can change quickly.

13.2 Designing for Change

The only constant in software engineering is change. Requirements shift, technologies evolve, and scale increases. Rigid architecture becomes brittle. The goal of a modern architect is not to predict the future, but to build a system that can adapt to it.

13.2.1 One-Way vs. Two-Way Doors

How do you know which decisions matter most? Amazon uses a powerful mental model: the distinction between **One-Way Doors** and **Two-Way Doors**.

- **Two-Way Doors** are reversible. If you walk through and dislike the outcome, you can step back. Examples include a linting rule, a variable name, or a minor UI component. Low reversal cost: decide quickly.
- **One-Way Doors** are irreversible (or very expensive to reverse). Once you pass through, you are committed for a long time. Examples include database paradigms (SQL vs. NoSQL), public APIs, or core language choices.

Architecture focuses on the One-Way Doors.

> **Note**
>
> The "Last Responsible Moment" means delaying an irreversible decision until the point where the cost of delay exceeds the cost of commitment. Decide when information is sufficient, not when fear demands certainty.

13.2.2 Fitness Functions and Guardrails

Evolutionary architecture succeeds by using guardrails that guide change safely. Fitness functions are automated checks that verify whether architecture still meets its goals as the system evolves. Use automated tests, performance budgets, SLOs, static analysis, and continuous integration to detect drift early and keep decisions honest.

13.3 Modularity and Boundaries

As systems grow, they tend toward chaos. Without discipline, a codebase becomes a "Big Ball of Mud" – a spaghetti mess where everything touches everything else. Modularity prevents this.

13.3.1 The Junk Drawer vs. The Utensil Tray

Imagine a kitchen junk drawer. It contains batteries, rubber bands, a screwdriver, and takeout menus. If you want to find a battery, you have to dig through everything. If you spill water in the drawer, everything gets wet.

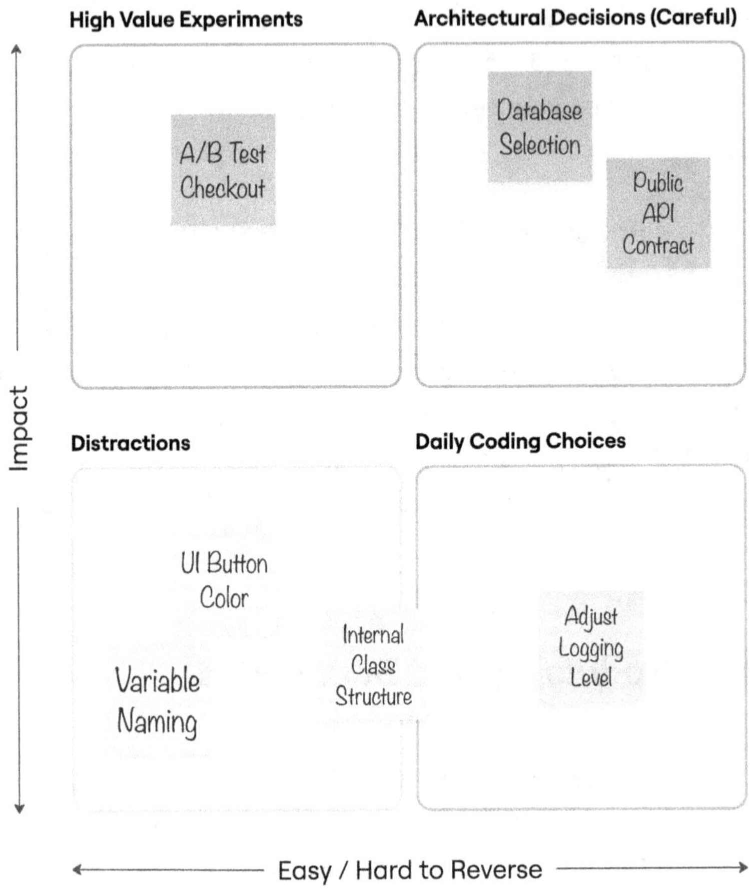

Figure 13.1: One-Way vs. Two-Way Doors – map reversibility and impact to decide quickly on reversible choices and deliberately on hard-to-reverse architecture decisions

Now imagine a utensil tray. Forks are in one slot, spoons in another, knives in a third. The boundaries are clear. You can take out all the spoons to wash them without touching the knives.

Software should be a utensil tray, not a junk drawer. We achieve this through **Separation of Concerns** and **Loose Coupling**.

- **Cohesion:** Things that change together should stay together (all spoons in one slot).
- **Coupling:** Components should know as little about each other as possible.

Separation of Concerns means each part has one primary responsibility; avoid mixing UI logic, domain rules, and data access in the same place.

> ⚠ Warning
>
> Beware of "Leaky Abstractions." If your Service layer returns a raw database object (like a SQLAlchemy row) to the UI, you have broken the boundary. The UI now depends on the database schema. Always convert data to a neutral format (DTO) before crossing boundaries.

> Note
>
> A DTO (Data Transfer Object) is a simple, neutral data shape used to cross boundaries without exposing internal domain or persistence types.

13.3.2 The Dependency Rule

In Clean Architecture, dependencies point inward. Business logic (the "Core") should not know about the database, web framework, or UI. Those are details. Details depend on policy, not the other way around.

If business logic imports `SQLAlchemy` or `React`, you lock yourself into those tools. If you instead depend on an interface, you remain free to swap implementations.

Example: Dependency Injection

Here is how we break tight coupling with Dependency Injection.

Tight Coupling (The Junk Drawer):

`PaymentProcessor` creates its own `StripeApi`. If we want to switch to PayPal or test without Stripe, we cannot.

```
# Bad: Hardcoded dependency
class StripeApi:
    def charge(self, amount: int):
        print(f"Charging {amount} via Stripe")

class PaymentProcessor:
    def __init__(self):
        # ⚠ Violation: The processor is glued to
        ↪ Stripe
        self.api = StripeApi()

    def process_order(self, amount: int):
        self.api.charge(amount)
```

Loose Coupling (The Utensil Tray):

`PaymentProcessor` asks for a `PaymentProvider`. It doesn't care if it's Stripe, PayPal, or a fake provider for testing.

```
# Good: Dependency Injection
from typing import Protocol

# 1. Define the "Shape" of the tool we need (The
↪  Interface)
class PaymentProvider(Protocol):
    def charge(self, amount: int) -> None:
        ...

class StripeProvider:
    def charge(self, amount: int):
        print(f"Charging {amount} via Stripe")

class FakeProvider:
    def charge(self, amount: int):
        print(f"Fake charge of {amount} for testing")

class PaymentProcessor:
    # 2. Inject the dependency
    def __init__(self, provider: PaymentProvider):
        self.provider = provider

    def process_order(self, amount: int):
        self.provider.charge(amount)

# Usage
real_service = PaymentProcessor(StripeProvider())
test_service = PaymentProcessor(FakeProvider())
```

Note

`PaymentProvider` uses `typing.Protocol` (Python 3.8+). On earlier versions, install `typing_extensions` and import `Protocol` from there.

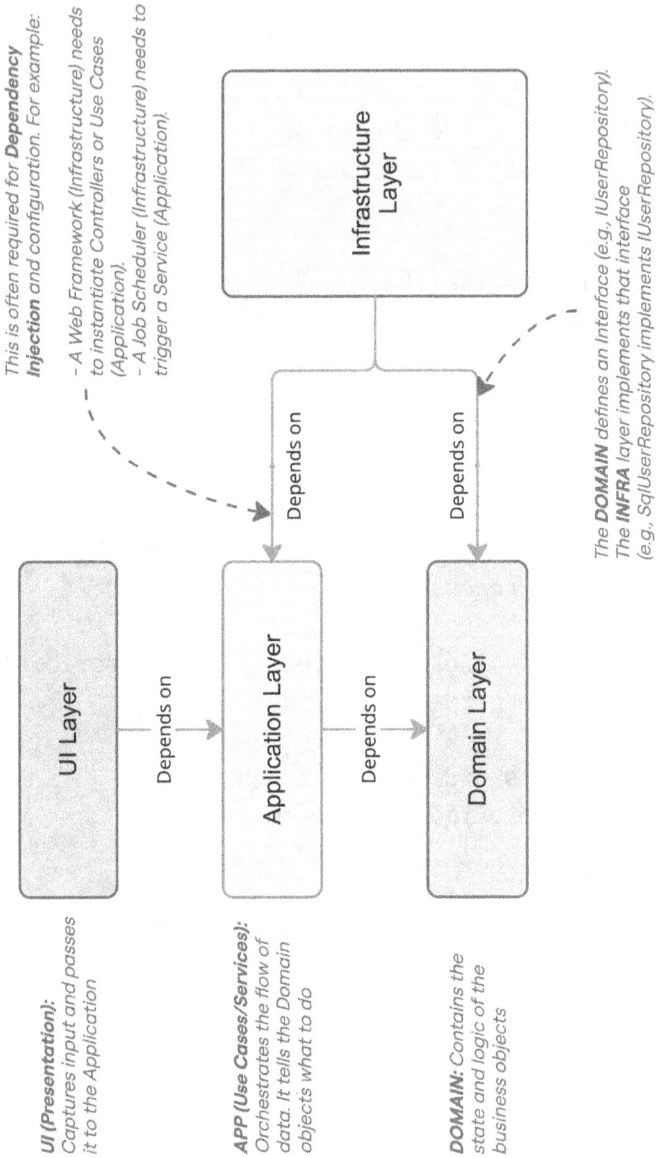

Figure 13.2: Clean Architecture dependency flow – dependencies point inward; Domain holds policy, Application orchestrates; UI depends on Application; Infrastructure implements details behind interfaces

> **Note**
>
> Infrastructure implements interfaces defined in the Domain layer, ensuring the Domain remains unaware of implementation details like databases or HTTP clients.

13.4 APIs as Contracts

When two modules interact, they need an agreement. In software, this agreement is the API (Application Programming Interface).

The Restaurant Menu

Think of an API as a restaurant menu.

1. **The Promise:** The menu lists "Cheeseburger." It promises that if you order it, you will receive a bun, meat, and cheese.
2. **Encapsulation:** The menu does *not* tell you how the chef cooks the burger, where they bought the meat, or what kind of spatula they use. You don't go into the kitchen to cook it yourself.
3. **Versioning:** If the restaurant wants to change the burger (e.g., make it vegan), they can't just silently swap it for everyone who ordered the classic one. They have to print a new menu or add a "Vegan Burger" item.

In code, your public interfaces are the menu. Once other teams (or other parts of your code) rely on them, you cannot break them.

Example: The API Contract

In TypeScript, we use `interfaces` to define the contract strictly.

```
// The Contract (The Menu)
// Consumers rely ONLY on this.
interface OrderService {
    placeOrder(itemId: string, quantity: number):
     ↪ Promise<boolean>;
    getOrderStatus(orderId: string): string;
}

// The Implementation (The Kitchen)
// This can change completely (e.g., from SQL to
 ↪ Redis)
// without breaking the code that calls it.
class SqlOrderService implements OrderService {
    async placeOrder(itemId: string, quantity:
     ↪ number): Promise<boolean> {
        console.log(`Inserting order for ${itemId}
         ↪ into SQL database...`);
        return true;
    }

    getOrderStatus(orderId: string): string {
        return "Processing";
    }
}

// The Consumer (The Customer)
function handleCheckout(service: OrderService, item:
 ↪ string) {
    // This function doesn't know it's using SQL.
    // It just knows the contract.
}
```

```
// Production-safe consumer should await the Promise
async function handleCheckoutSafe(service:
↪ OrderService, item: string): Promise<void> {
    await service.placeOrder(item, 1);
}
```

Public APIs are often one-way doors for external consumers. Prefer additive changes and mark old behaviors deprecated with a clear sunset window.

```
// Non-breaking evolution via deprecation
interface OrderServiceV2 extends OrderService {
    /** @deprecated Use getOrder(id) which returns
    ↪ more detail */
    getOrderStatus(orderId: string): string;
    getOrder(orderId: string): { id: string; status:
    ↪ string };
}
```

> **Note**
>
> Use semantic versioning for public APIs and honor a clear deprecation window (for example, support for N releases) before removing deprecated endpoints or behaviors.

13.5 Domain-Driven Design (The "Why")

Architecture is not just technical patterns; it is about solving business problems. Domain-Driven Design (DDD) says: *Model the software to match the real world.*

Speaking the Native Language

Imagine a developer talking to a logistics expert.

- **Developer:** "I'll update the `transfer_batch_row` in the `shipping_table`."
- **Expert:** "You mean you're scheduling a Shipment?"

If the code says `TransferBatch` but the business says `Shipment`, bugs hide in translation. You misunderstand requirements because you speak different languages.

- **Ubiquitous Language:** Use the exact same terms in your code (class names, variables) as the experts use in conversation.
- **Bounded Contexts:** Words have different meanings in different contexts. To a "Sales" team, a `Customer` is someone with a lead score and a probability to buy. To a "Support" team, a `Customer` is someone with a ticket history and a service level agreement. Don't try to create one giant `Customer` class that does everything. Create a `SalesCustomer` context and a `SupportCustomer` context.

Start small: use lightweight DDD to name core concepts and carve boundaries; deepen the model only where complexity and change justify the investment.

13.6 The Law of Trade-offs

There is no perfect architecture. There is no "best" database or framework. Only trade-offs.

> **Note**
>
> If you find an article titled "Why X is better than Y" without a "Context" or "Downsides" section, treat it with suspicion.

Every architectural choice has a cost:

- **Microservices** provide organizational scale but add massive network complexity.
- **Traditional SQL** offers consistency but makes horizontal scaling harder.
- **NoSQL** grants flexibility but sacrifices complex joins.

The senior engineer's job is not to pick the "coolest" tech, but to pick the option where benefits outweigh costs *for this problem*.

13.7 Documenting the "Why"

Because architecture involves trade-offs, you must document *why* you chose a path.

Six months from now, you (or a successor) may ask, "Why did we use a graph database for a simple blog?"

If you do not write it down, people may assume incompetence. If you record, "We expected a social feature that never launched," they understand.

Use **Architecture Decision Records** (ADRs). An ADR is a short text file stored in your repo that captures:

1. **Context:** What was the problem?
2. **Decision:** What did we choose?
3. **Alternatives:** What did we reject?
4. **Consequences:** What are the pros and cons we accepted?

```
# ADR-001: Use PostgreSQL for Core Data

### Context
We need a reliable, ACID-compliant database for
↪ financial transactions.

### Decision
We will use PostgreSQL 15.

### Status
Accepted

### Date
2025-11-27

### Alternatives Considered
- MySQL: Familiar team skills but weaker JSON features
↪ for our use case
- MongoDB: Flexible schema but weaker transactional
↪ guarantees for money flows

### Consequences
+ Strong data consistency
+ Rich ecosystem
- Harder to scale horizontally than NoSQL
```

This prevents "Chesterton's Fence" – tearing down code because you do not see why it exists.

13.8 Conclusion

Architecture is thought made visible. It is the art of drawing lines – boundaries that separate volatile from stable, policy from detail.

Remember:

1. Distinguish between One-Way and Two-Way doors.
2. Keep your "kitchen" (implementation) separate from your "menu" (interface).
3. Speak the language of the business.
4. Document your trade-offs.

A good architecture not only makes the system work today; it makes it a joy to change tomorrow.

Next, we explore how to keep that system running when things inevitably go wrong. *Chapter 14 (Pillar 5 – Reliability and Resilience)*.

Chapter 14:

Pillar 5 – Reliability and Resilience

Reliability is the promise you intend to keep; **resilience** is how you keep it when the world misbehaves.

14.1 The "Perfect Code" Fallacy

Imagine you've just deployed a new payment service. The code is clean, the unit tests pass with 100% coverage, and the architecture diagrams are pristine. You go to sleep confident.

At 3:00 AM, your phone buzzes. The entire checkout flow is down.

Why? A third-party tax calculation API – one you don't control – started timing out. Your service waited for each request until it hit the default 60-second timeout. Threads piled up, memory spiked, and eventually, your perfectly written service crashed.

This is the hard truth of **distributed systems**: **You cannot code your way out of failure.**

Resilience is an architectural concern (*Chapter 13 (Pillar 4 – Architecture and Design)*). Patterns like **Circuit Breakers** and **Bulk-**

heads are one-way doors – much easier to build in from the start than to retrofit. In a modern system, failure is not an anomaly; it is a statistical certainty. Networks glitch, disks fill up, and dependencies go dark. The difference between a fragile system and a robust one isn't the absence of errors – it's the ability to absorb them without collapsing.

This chapter explores **Reliability** (doing what you said you would) and **Resilience** (surviving the inevitable shocks), transforming "it works on my machine" into "it stays up in production."

> Note
>
> Quick definitions.
>
> - **Reliability:** The consistency of a system in meeting its intended behavior over time.
> - **Resilience:** The ability of a system to withstand failures, degrade gracefully, and recover quickly.

14.2 High Availability vs. Fault Tolerance

Junior engineers often use these terms interchangeably, but they represent different strategies for keeping the lights on.

14.2.1 The Tire Analogy

Think about driving a car.

- **High Availability (HA)** is like having a **spare tire** in the trunk. If you get a flat, you stop, swap it out, and you're back on the road in 15 minutes. The interruption is brief but noticeable.

In software, this looks like a **load balancer** detecting a dead server and routing traffic to a healthy one.

- **Fault Tolerance (FT)** is like having **run-flat tires**. You get a puncture, but the car keeps moving. You might have to drive slower (**graceful degradation**), but you reach your destination without stopping. In software, this looks like a video streaming service lowering resolution when bandwidth drops, rather than showing an error screen.

14.2.2 The Language of Reliability: SLIs, SLOs, and SLAs

To build reliable systems, you must first define what "reliable" means. We use three acronyms to quantify this:

1. **SLI (Service Level Indicator)**: The metric you measure. (e.g., "The latency of HTTP requests.")
2. **SLO (Service Level Objective)**: The target you aim for. (e.g., "99.9% of requests complete in under 200ms.") This is an internal engineering goal.
3. **SLA (Service Level Agreement)**: The promise you make to customers (and the penalty if you break it). (e.g., "If availability drops below 99.9%, we refund 10% of your bill.")

> **Note**
>
> You should care deeply about SLOs. SLAs are for lawyers; SLOs are for engineers. If you consistently miss your SLO, you are burning user trust.

14.2.3 The Cost of Nines

What's the real difference between 99.9% and 99.99% availability? More than you think. Each "nine" you add exponentially increases complexity and cost. Your SLO must be a conscious business decision, not a vanity metric.

Table 14.1: Availability levels and their downtime impact

Availability %	Downtime per Year	Downtime per Week
99% ("two nines")	3.65 days	1.68 hours
99.9% ("three nines")	8.77 hours	10.1 minutes
99.99% ("four nines")	52.6 minutes	1.01 minutes
99.999% ("five nines")	5.26 minutes	6.05 seconds

Achieving "five nines" requires multi-region failover, automated recovery, and a massive engineering investment. Is your service critical enough to justify it, or is the 8.77 hours of downtime from "three nines" acceptable for your users? Choose the simplest solution that meets the business need.

> Note
>
> **Error budget** connects reliability to delivery speed. If your SLO is 99.9% availability, your error budget is 0.1% downtime. Spend it on safe change (releases); pause when it's exhausted.

14.3 Resiliency Patterns: The Safety Nets

If failure is inevitable, how do we stop it from cascading? We use architectural patterns designed to contain damage.

Note

The "Fail Fast" Principle
A core tenet of resilience is to **fail fast**. It is better to return an immediate, clear error than to hang indefinitely. Slow failures consume resources, block callers, and create ambiguity, making a bad situation worse. The patterns in this section are all designed to enforce this principle.

14.3.1 The Circuit Breaker

In your home, if a toaster shorts out, a circuit breaker trips. It cuts power to that specific outlet to prevent the wiring in the walls from catching fire.

In software, a **Circuit Breaker** wraps a dangerous operation (like a network call). If calls start failing repeatedly, the breaker "trips" (opens). Subsequent calls fail immediately without hitting the struggling dependency, giving it time to recover. This embodies the principle of **failing fast**: it is better to return a clear, immediate error than to hang indefinitely, confusing users and blocking system resources.

Example: Circuit Breaker in Python

This Python example uses a decorator to implement a simple circuit breaker.

```
import time
import functools

class CircuitBreakerOpenException(Exception):
    pass
```

```
class CircuitBreaker:
    def __init__(self, failure_threshold=3,
    ↪   recovery_timeout=10):
        self.failure_threshold = failure_threshold
        self.recovery_timeout = recovery_timeout
        self.failures = 0
        self.last_failure_time = 0
        self.state = "CLOSED"  # CLOSED (working),
        ↪   OPEN (broken), HALF-OPEN (testing)

    def __call__(self, func):
        @functools.wraps(func)
        def wrapper(*args, **kwargs):
            if self.state == "OPEN":
                # Check if enough time has passed to
                ↪   try again
                if time.time() -
                ↪   self.last_failure_time >
                ↪   self.recovery_timeout:
                    self.state = "HALF-OPEN"
                else:
                    raise CircuitBreakerOpenException(
                        "Circuit is OPEN. Call
                        ↪   rejected.")

            try:
                result = func(*args, **kwargs)
                # Success! Reset the breaker if it was
                ↪   struggling
                if self.state == "HALF-OPEN":
                    self.state = "CLOSED"
                    self.failures = 0
                return result
            except Exception as e:
                self.failures += 1
```

```
                self.last_failure_time = time.time()
                if self.failures >=
                ↪ self.failure_threshold:
                    self.state = "OPEN"
                raise e
        return wrapper

# Usage
@CircuitBreaker(failure_threshold=2,
↪ recovery_timeout=5)
def call_unreliable_api():
    # Simulate a network call that might fail
    print("Calling API...")
    raise ConnectionError("API Timeout")

# The first two calls will try and fail.
# The third call will be rejected immediately by the
↪ breaker.
```

The state transitions of a circuit breaker are critical to understanding its behavior (see Figure 14.1)

14.3.2 Retries with Exponential Backoff

When a network call fails, your instinct might be to try again immediately. If thousands of users do this simultaneously, you create a **retry storm**, effectively overwhelming your own service.

The solution is **Exponential Backoff**: wait a short time, then retry. If it fails again, wait twice as long.

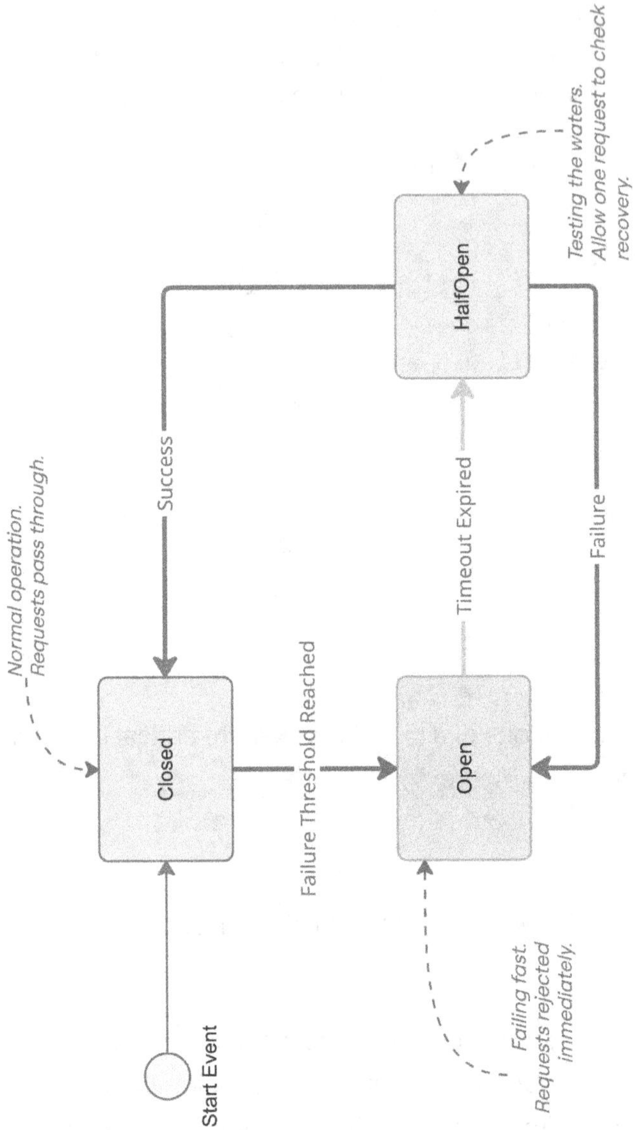

Figure 14.1: Circuit breaker state transitions – CLOSED (healthy), OPEN (trip on repeated failures), HALF-OPEN (probe for recovery); fail fast, then cautiously test before resuming

> ⚠ Warning
>
> Always add **jitter** (randomness) to your backoff delays. If all clients retry at exactly 1s, 2s, 4s, they will still hit the server in synchronized waves. Jitter spreads the load.

> Note
>
> **When NOT to Retry**
> **Retry** is a pattern for transient, temporary failures. Retrying certain errors will only make things worse. Never retry:
>
> - **Client Errors (4xx status codes):** A `400 Bad Request` or `403 Forbidden` error won't be fixed by trying again. The request itself is flawed.
> - **Non-Idempotent Operations:** Retrying a `POST /create-user` request that succeeded but failed to return a response could create duplicate users. Use **idempotency** keys to make such operations safe to retry.
> - **Long-Running Operations that Timed Out:** If an operation timed out on the client side, it might still be running on the server. Retrying could trigger duplicate work.

Example: Robust Retries in C#

This C# example demonstrates a retry policy with exponential backoff and jitter. While libraries like `Polly` are standard for this, understanding the logic is key.

```
using System;
using System.Threading.Tasks;
```

```
public class RetryPolicy
{
    private readonly int _maxRetries;
    private readonly Random _jitter;

    public RetryPolicy(int maxRetries)
    {
        _maxRetries = maxRetries;
        _jitter = new Random();
    }

    public async Task<T> ExecuteAsync<T>(Func<Task<T>>
    ↪  operation)
    {
        int attempt = 0;
        while (true)
        {
            try
            {
                return await operation();
            }
            catch (Exception ex)
            {
                attempt++;
                if (attempt > _maxRetries)
                {
                    // If we've exceeded max retries,
                    ↪  re-throw the last exception
                    throw;
                }

                // Exponential backoff: 2^attempt
                ↪  seconds (e.g., 2, 4, 8...)
                var delay = Math.Pow(2, attempt);
```

```
                    // Add jitter: +/- 20% random
                    ↪   variation
                    var jitter = _jitter.NextDouble() *
                    ↪   (delay * 0.4) - (delay * 0.2);
                    var finalDelay =
                    ↪   TimeSpan.FromSeconds(delay +
                    ↪   jitter);

                    Console.WriteLine($"Attempt {attempt}
↪   failed: {ex.Message}. Retrying in
↪   {finalDelay.TotalSeconds:F2}s...");
                    await Task.Delay(finalDelay);
                }
            }
        }
}
```

Note

Catching Specific Exceptions

For clarity, the code examples in this chapter catch a broad `Exception`. In a production system, this is an anti-pattern. Your resilience policies should only handle specific, transient exceptions that are safe to retry (e.g., `HttpRequestException`, `TimeoutException`, or HTTP 503 errors). Catching everything risks hiding programming bugs (like `NullReferenceException`) and retrying non-retriable failures, making problems worse.

Timeouts

Retries without **timeout** are a trap. A call that never times out will hold resources (threads, memory) indefinitely and amplify incidents. Always set explicit, context-appropriate **timeouts** on external calls, and ensure your retry backoff respects those limits to avoid long-tail latency.

14.3.3 Bulkheads

Ships are divided into watertight compartments called bulkheads. If the hull is breached, water fills only one section, and the ship stays afloat.

In software, **Bulkheads** isolate resources. You might have separate thread pools for your “User Profile” service and your “Image Processing” service. If image processing hangs and consumes all its threads, the user profile service remains unaffected.

14.3.4 When Patterns Aren’t Enough: Backup and DR

Resiliency patterns handle runtime failures, but they can’t save you from data corruption or a full datacenter outage. For that, you need a plan for Backup and Disaster Recovery (DR).

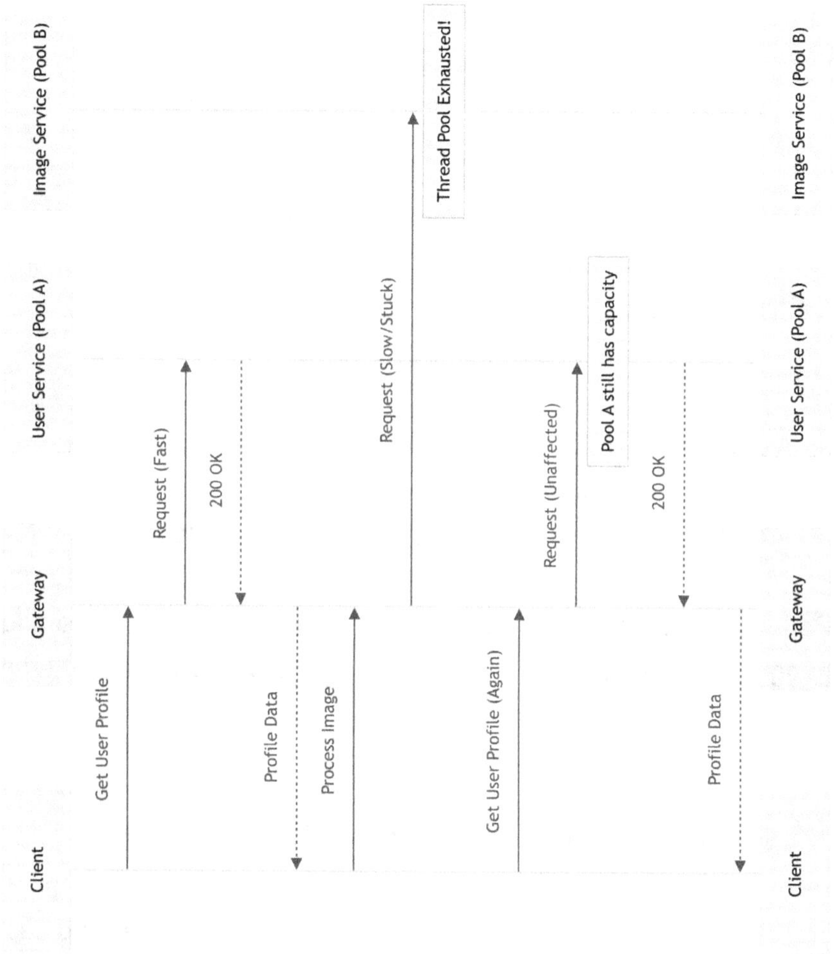

Figure 14.2: Bulkheads isolate resources – separate pools prevent a failing service from exhausting shared capacity; damage stays contained and critical paths remain available

Two key metrics define your DR strategy:

- **RTO (Recovery Time Objective)**: How quickly must you be back online after a disaster? (e.g., 1 hour)
- **RPO (Recovery Point Objective)**: How much data can you afford to lose? (e.g., 15 minutes of transactions)

A low RTO/RPO is expensive, requiring hot standbys in different geographic regions. A high RTO/RPO might be as simple as restoring a nightly backup.

> ⚠ Warning
>
> A **backup** you haven't tested is not a backup; it's a comforting lie. Regularly conduct restore drills to ensure your backups are valid and your team knows the recovery procedure.

Patterns protect runtime behavior; disasters target persistence and geography. Backup and DR address risks that resilience patterns cannot.

14.4 Observability as Reliability's Co-pilot

You now have three powerful patterns: Circuit Breakers stop cascading failures, Retries handle transient glitches, and Bulkheads contain damage. But here's the uncomfortable question: how do you *know* they work?

This is where the **Observability** pillar (*Chapter 12 (Pillar 3 Observability – Building Systems You Can See and Understand)*) becomes critical. Your resilience patterns must be instrumented.

- **Metrics:** Is the circuit breaker open? How many retries are happening per minute?
- **Logs:** Why did the retry fail? What was the error?
- **Traces:** Which downstream service is causing the latency that tripped the breaker?

Without observability, your safety nets are invisible. You can't tune them, and you'll only discover they're misconfigured during a real outage.

> **Note**
>
> SLIs require instrumentation. If latency, errors, and saturation aren't measured, SLO adherence is unknowable – and reliability becomes hope instead of engineering.

14.5 Chaos Engineering: Testing the Safety Nets

You have circuit breakers and bulkheads. You have observability. But do they work together?

Chaos Engineering is the discipline of experimenting on a system to build confidence in its ability to withstand turbulent conditions. It is not about "breaking things in production" randomly; it is about **controlled experiments**.

14.5.1 The Fire Drill Analogy

We don't wait for a real fire to test if the alarms work and if people know where the exits are. We conduct fire drills.

Chaos Engineering is a fire drill for your code. You might:

1. **Hypothesize:** "If the recommendation engine slows down, the homepage should still load (just without recommendations)."
2. **Inject Failure:** Artificially add 5 seconds of latency to the recommendation service.
3. **Observe:** Does the homepage load? Did the circuit breaker trip? Did the monitoring alerts fire?
4. **Learn:** If the homepage crashed, you have a reliability gap to fix.

> **Further Reading**
>
> Chaos experiments complement the Testing Pyramid as system-level validation. See *Chapter 8 (The Testing Pyramid)* for how unit, integration, and E2E tests provide fast feedback during development.

14.5.2 Reliability Readiness Checklist

Before you ship or change a critical path, ask:

- ☐ **Timeouts set?** Every external call has a bounded wait.
- ☐ **Retries safe?** Idempotent operations only, with backoff + jitter.
- ☐ **Circuit breaker in place?** Fails fast on repeated dependency errors.
- ☐ **Bulkheads defined?** Resource isolation prevents one pool exhausting all capacity.
- ☐ **Fallbacks / degradation?** Non-critical features can gracefully drop.
- ☐ **Metrics + traces?** SLIs (latency, errors, saturation) are instrumented.

- ☐ **Alerts calibrated?** Actionable thresholds tied to SLOs, not noise.
- ☐ **Error budget monitored?** Release velocity pauses when burn rate spikes.
- ☐ **Backups tested?** Recent restore drill passed; RPO/RTO still valid.
- ☐ **Chaos scenarios rehearsed?** At least one failure injection validated assumptions.

14.6 Conclusion

Reliability is not an accident; it is a design choice. By accepting that failure is inevitable, you shift your focus from "preventing errors" to "managing impact."

You now have the tools – SLOs to set targets, patterns like Circuit Breakers, Timeouts, Retries, and Bulkheads to contain faults, and Chaos Engineering to verify your defenses.

Resilient systems keep running when dependencies fail. But what happens when the *data* those systems depend on is corrupted, outdated, or inconsistent? *Chapter 15 (Pillar 6 – Data and Knowledge Management)* shows how to treat data with the same defensive rigor you now apply to runtime failures.

Chapter 15:

Pillar 6 – Data and Knowledge Management

> **Note**
>
> Data is the longest-lived part of any system. Code is transient; data is forever.

In the early days of a startup, the database is often treated like a magical bucket. You throw JSON blobs or rows into it, and they stick. Speed is the only metric that matters. But as the system grows, that bucket starts to look less like a well-organized archive and more like a swamp.

Imagine a team where the database is a "mystery box." Engineers are afraid to touch a specific table because "it might break something," but no one knows exactly what. A column named `status_v2` sits next to `status_new` and `status_final`, and the only person who knew the difference left two years ago.

This is the reality of **Data Gravity**. As data accumulates, it becomes heavier, harder to move, and harder to change. Applications and services orbit around it, pulled into its implementation details. If you treat data as a passive byproduct of your code, it will eventually become a liability that freezes your architecture in place.

This chapter explores how to treat data with the same engineering rigor we apply to code: defining contracts, managing lifecycles, and ensuring it remains a valuable asset rather than a toxic swamp.

15.1 Data as a Product

The most common mistake junior engineers make is viewing the database as a private storage locker for their application. They change a schema, deploy the code, and assume everything is fine. But in a distributed system, data is rarely private. It is consumed by analytics pipelines, other microservices, and reporting dashboards.

Think of the difference between a **Public Library** and a **Hoarder's Attic**.

- A **Library** has a catalog (metadata), strict rules for checking books in and out (contracts), and a librarian who ensures everything is in the right place (governance).
- A **Hoarder's Attic** has piles of stuff. Some of it might be valuable, but good luck finding it. There are no rules, no catalog, and no guarantees that what you find isn't broken.

To move from the attic to the library, we must treat data as a **Product**.

Data Contracts. Just as we define APIs for our services (REST, gRPC), we must define APIs for our data. A Data Contract is an agreement between the data producer and its consumers. It explicitly states:

- **Schema**: What fields exist, and what are their types?
- **Semantics**: What does "`status: 3`" actually mean?
- **SLAs**: How fresh is this data? How often is it updated?

When you treat data as a product, you stop exposing your internal database schema directly to the world. Instead, you expose a stable interface. This is the distinction between **Data on the Inside** (your private implementation, optimized for storage) and **Data on the Outside** (your public contract, optimized for consumption). This concept aligns closely with the **DTO (Data Transfer Object)** pattern and **Anti-Corruption Layers** discussed in *Chapter 13 (Pillar 4 – Architecture and Design)*.

Example: Enforcing Data Contracts

In a TypeScript service, we can use a library like Zod to strictly enforce the shape of data we accept and produce, rejecting anything that doesn't fit the contract. This prevents "data pollution" where bad data sneaks into the system and breaks downstream consumers.

```
// intent: define and enforce a strict data contract
↪  for a user profile update
import { z } from 'zod';

// Define the contract (Schema)
const UserProfileSchema = z.object({
  userId: z.string().uuid(),
  email: z.string().email(),
  preferences: z.object({
    theme: z.enum(['light', 'dark', 'system']),
    notifications: z.boolean(),
  }),
  // Explicitly reject unknown fields to prevent
  ↪  "pollution"
```

```
}).strict();

type UserProfile = z.infer<typeof UserProfileSchema>;

function updateUserProfile(input: unknown):
↪ UserProfile {
  // Validate input against the contract
  const result = UserProfileSchema.safeParse(input);

  if (!result.success) {
    // Fail fast if the contract is violated
    throw new Error(`Data Contract Violation:
    ↪ ${result.error.message}`);
  }

  // Now we can safely treat 'result.data' as a valid
  ↪ Product
  return result.data;
}
```

15.2 Schema Evolution: The Time Dimension

Code changes instantly; you deploy a new binary, and the old logic is gone. Data, however, has a **history**. You cannot simply “refactor” a database table with millions of rows in the same way you rename a variable in your IDE.

Changing a schema in a live system is like **renovating a train station while the trains are still running**. You cannot stop the traffic. You must build the new platforms, divert the passengers, and demolish the old structures, only then.

The "Expand and Contract" Pattern

The industry standard for zero-downtime schema migrations is the **Expand and Contract** (or Parallel Change) pattern. It decouples the database change from the code deployment.

The process has three distinct phases:

1. **Expand**: Add the new column or table. The code writes to *both* the old and new locations but reads from the old.
2. **Migrate**: Backfill historical data to the new location. Switch the code to read from the new location (while still writing to both, just in case).
3. **Contract**: Stop writing to the old location. Remove the old column or table.

Example: Expand and Contract in Python

Here is how you might implement the logic for the "Expand" phase in a Python application using an ORM style.

```
# intent: demonstrate the 'Expand' phase where we
↪  write to both old and new columns
class User:
    def __init__(self, full_name, first_name=None,
    ↪  last_name=None):
        self.full_name = full_name  # The old column
        ↪  (deprecated)
        self.first_name = first_name # The new column
        self.last_name = last_name   # The new column

    def save(self):
        """
        Writes data to the database.
```

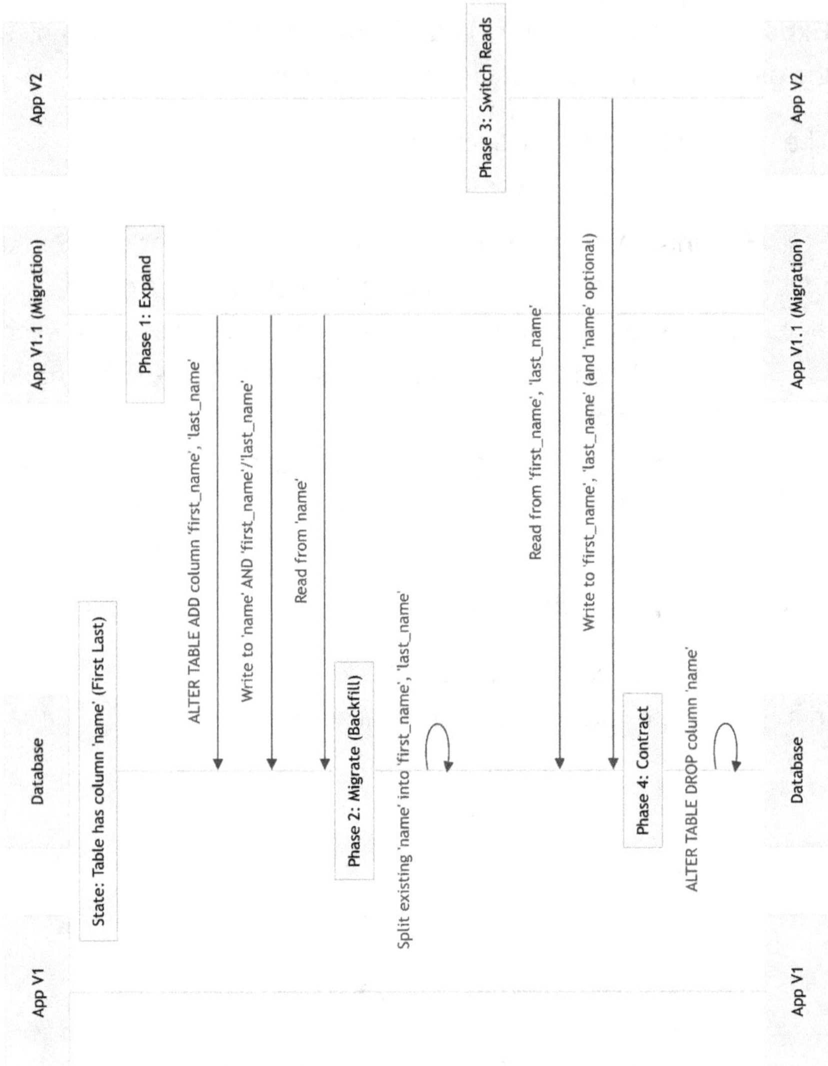

Figure 15.1: Expand-and-Contract schema migration – Expand: write to old and new; Migrate: backfill and switch reads; Contract: stop legacy writes and remove old structures for zero-downtime change

```
        During the transition phase, we must populate
↪   BOTH schema versions.
        """
        # Logic to split the old format into the new
        ↪   format
        # NOTE: This logic is temporary! It only
        ↪   exists during the migration phase.
        # Once the migration is complete (Phase 3),
        ↪   this code will be deleted.
        if self.full_name and not (self.first_name and
        ↪   self.last_name):
            parts = self.full_name.split(' ', 1)
            self.first_name = parts[0]
            self.last_name = parts[1] if len(parts) >
            ↪   1 else ''

        # Logic to maintain backward compatibility
        ↪   (construct old format from new)
        if (self.first_name or self.last_name) and not
        ↪   self.full_name:
            self.full_name = f"{self.first_name}
            ↪   {self.last_name}".strip()

        # Perform the DB write (pseudo-code)
        # db.execute("INSERT INTO users (full_name,
        ↪   first_name, last_name) ...")
        print(f"Persisting: Old='{self.full_name}',
        ↪   New='{self.first_name},
        ↪   {self.last_name}'")

# Usage
user = User(full_name="Grace Hopper")
user.save()
# Output: Persisting: Old='Grace Hopper', New='Grace,
↪   Hopper'
```

15.3 Metadata and Governance: The Map

If data is a product, **Metadata** is the packaging and the user manual. Without metadata, your data lake is just a swamp of unknown files.

Imagine trying to navigate a new city without a map, street signs, or GPS. That is what it feels like to join a company with poor data governance. You see a table called `transactions`, but you don't know:

- Who owns it?
- Is it up to date?
- Can I delete this row, or will it break the CEO's dashboard?

15.3.1 Data Catalogs and Lineage

A **Data Catalog** is the "city map" for your data. It allows engineers to discover datasets, understand their schemas, and see who owns them.

Data Lineage takes this a step further. It visualizes the flow of data through your system. It answers the question: "If I change the schema of the `User` table, what downstream reports will break?"

In the Figure 15.2, the lineage graph makes it obvious that a breaking change in the `User Service DB` will propagate through the ETL job and ultimately crash both the `Executive Dashboard` and the `Fraud Detection Model`. Without this visibility, the database team might assume their change is safe, only to cause a silent failure in a critical business report days later.

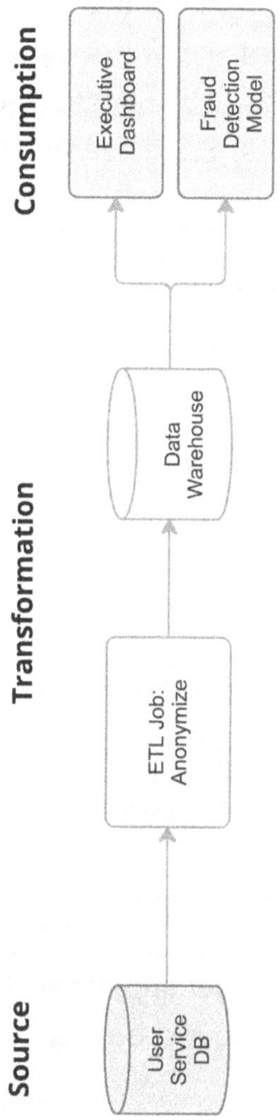

Figure 15.2: Data lineage – visualize source → transform → consume so upstream schema changes reveal downstream blast radius (ETL, dashboards, models) before they break production

15.3.2 Compliance as Code

Governance is also about safety and legality. Regulations like GDPR or CCPA require us to know exactly where Personally Identifiable Information (PII) lives. If you treat compliance as a metadata problem – tagging fields as `pii:true` or `retention:30-days` – you can automate enforcement.

For example, in a Protobuf or GraphQL schema, this might look like a comment annotation:

```
message User {
  string id = 1;
  string email = 2;  // @pii - Tagged for automated
   ↪  scrubbing
}
```

You can then build tools that automatically delete old data or mask PII in logs, rather than relying on manual audits.

15.4 Conclusion

Data is not just a detail of your implementation – it is the lifeblood of your system. It outlives your code, your servers, and often your tenure at the company.

- Treat data as a **Product** with explicit contracts and owners.
- Manage **Schema Evolution** carefully, decoupling structure changes from code deployments.
- Invest in **Metadata and Lineage** so you aren't wandering blindly through a swamp.

When you respect the gravity of data, you build systems that can evolve and grow without collapsing under their own weight.

Data is the foundation, but people build the house. Next, *Chapter 16 (Pillar 7 – Collaboration and Culture)* explores how to foster the human systems that keep your engineering practice alive and thriving.

Chapter 16:

Pillar 7 – Collaboration and Culture

> Note
>
> "The best code is meaningless if no one else can work with it."

In previous chapters, we discussed the technical pillars: Lifecycle, Security, Observability, Architecture, Reliability, and Data. These are the *mechanics* of engineering. However, a final pillar determines whether those mechanics work in practice: **Collaboration**.

Engineering is a team sport. The days of the "lone genius" hacker who locks themselves in a basement and emerges with a perfect system are over – if they ever existed. Modern systems are too complex for one person to hold in their head.

This chapter explores the **human infrastructure** of software engineering. We will look at how to build a culture of shared ownership, how to treat documentation as a living system, how to use code review for knowledge transfer, and how to learn from failure without blaming individuals.

16.1 The Myth of the Lone Genius

Imagine a brilliant engineer named Alex. Alex writes complex, highly optimized code and knows every corner of the system. They are the "go-to" person for every outage. But Alex works alone. They don't write documentation because "it's all in the code," and they view code reviews as a nuisance.

One day, Alex leaves the company.

Suddenly, the system becomes a "black box." The remaining team is terrified to touch it. Simple bugs become major incidents because no one understands the architecture. Development velocity grinds to a halt.

Alex's brilliance was actually a liability. By failing to collaborate, they built a **Bus Factor of 1** – a system that is one accident away from being unmaintainable.

True seniority is not about how much code you write, but how much you enable others to write.

16.2 Engineering Culture: The Invisible Foundation

Culture is like soil. You can plant the best seeds (hire the most talented engineers), but if the soil is toxic, nothing will grow.

A healthy engineering culture is not about free snacks or ping-pong tables; it is about **how you work together when things get hard**. It is built on a few core principles:

16.2.1 Psychological Safety

Google's "Project Aristotle" found that the number one predictor of high-performing teams was psychological safety: the belief that you won't be punished or humiliated for speaking up with ideas, questions, concerns, or mistakes.

In a safe team, a junior engineer can say, "I don't understand why we're doing it this way," without fear of being ridiculed. This openness catches design flaws early and fosters learning.

16.2.2 Stewardship over Ownership

"Ownership" implies possession: "This is *my* code."

"Stewardship" implies caretaking: "I am responsible for this code, but I build it for the team."

Stewards write documentation. Stewards write tests. Stewards make their code readable because they know that one day, someone else will have to maintain it.

16.2.3 Blamelessness

When things go wrong (and they will), a toxic culture asks, "Who broke it?" A healthy culture asks, "How did the system allow this to happen?" We will explore this deeper in the section on Postmortems.

16.2.4 Code Example: Culture as Code

You can codify your culture in your repository. A `TEAM_CHARTER.md` or `CONTRIBUTING.md` file sets explicit expectations for how the team collaborates.

```
# Team Charter: The Velocity Squad

### Our Values

1.  **Leave it better than you found it.** (Boy Scout Rule)
2.  **Drafts are welcome.** Share work early to get feedback on direction.
3.  **Questions are free.** There is no such thing as a "dumb question."

### Code Review Norms

-   **Review within 24 hours.** Unblocking teammates is higher priority than writing new code.
-   **Nitpicks are optional.** Prefix minor style comments with `(nit)` so the author knows they are not blocking.
-   **Praise good work.** Code review is also for celebrating clever solutions.
```

16.3 Documentation as a Living System

16.3.1 The 15-Minute Rule

Documentation is often treated as an afterthought – a chore to be done "if we have time" (which we never do). This leads to the "Write-Once, Read-Never" problem, where wikis become graveyards of outdated information.

We must treat documentation **as code**. It should be versioned, reviewed, and automated where possible.

Use this simple heuristic for when to write docs: **If it takes more than 15 minutes to explain a concept to a new team member, write it down.**

If you explain it verbally, you have to explain it again to the next person. If you write it down, you scale your knowledge infinitely.

16.3.2 Types of Living Documentation

1. The README

The `README.md` is the front door to your project. It should answer three questions in 5 minutes:

1. What does this project do?
2. How do I run it locally?
3. How do I deploy it?

2. Architectural Decision Records (ADRs)

Why did we choose PostgreSQL over MongoDB? Why are we using a microservices architecture here?

Memory is faulty. Six months from now, you will forget *why* you made a decision. An **ADR** captures the context, the options considered, and the final decision. It is a time capsule for your future self.

Example: ADR Template

```
# ADR 001: Use Redis for Session Caching

**Status:** Accepted
**Date:** 2023-10-27
**Context:**
```

```
Our current in-memory session storage prevents us from
↪   scaling the API horizontally.
We need a distributed caching solution.

**Options Considered:**

1.   **Sticky Sessions:** Low effort, but leads to
↪   uneven load balancing.
2.   **Database (PostgreSQL):** High latency for
↪   session reads.
3.   **Redis:** Low latency, supports expiration, but
↪   adds infrastructure complexity.

**Decision:**

We will use **Redis**.

**Consequences:**

-    (+) We can scale API instances statelessly.
-    (-) We need to manage a Redis cluster.
-    (-) We must handle Redis connection failures
↪   gracefully.
```

3. Auto-Generated API Docs

The best documentation lives close to the code. For APIs, use tools that generate documentation from your code comments and type definitions.

- **Python:** Use Docstrings and Sphinx/MkDocs.
- **TypeScript:** Use JSDoc and TypeDoc.
- **OpenAPI (Swagger):** Generate specs directly from your route handlers.

```
# intent: demonstrate self-documenting code using
↪   Python docstrings
from fastapi import FastAPI
from pydantic import BaseModel

app = FastAPI()

class User(BaseModel):
    username: str
    email: str

@app.post("/users/", response_model=User,
↪   summary="Create a new user")
def create_user(user: User):
    """
    Creates a new user in the system.

    - **username**: Must be unique.
    - **email**: Must be a valid email format.

    Returns the created user object with its assigned
↪   ID.
    """
    return user
```

This code *is* the documentation. It cannot get out of sync because if you change the code, the docs update automatically.

> **Note**
>
> This principle applies universally. In C#, you would use XML comments (`///`) to generate Swagger UI. In Java, Javadoc. The tool changes, but the principle of keeping docs close to the code remains.

Documentation has a lifecycle, just like code. See Figure 16.1

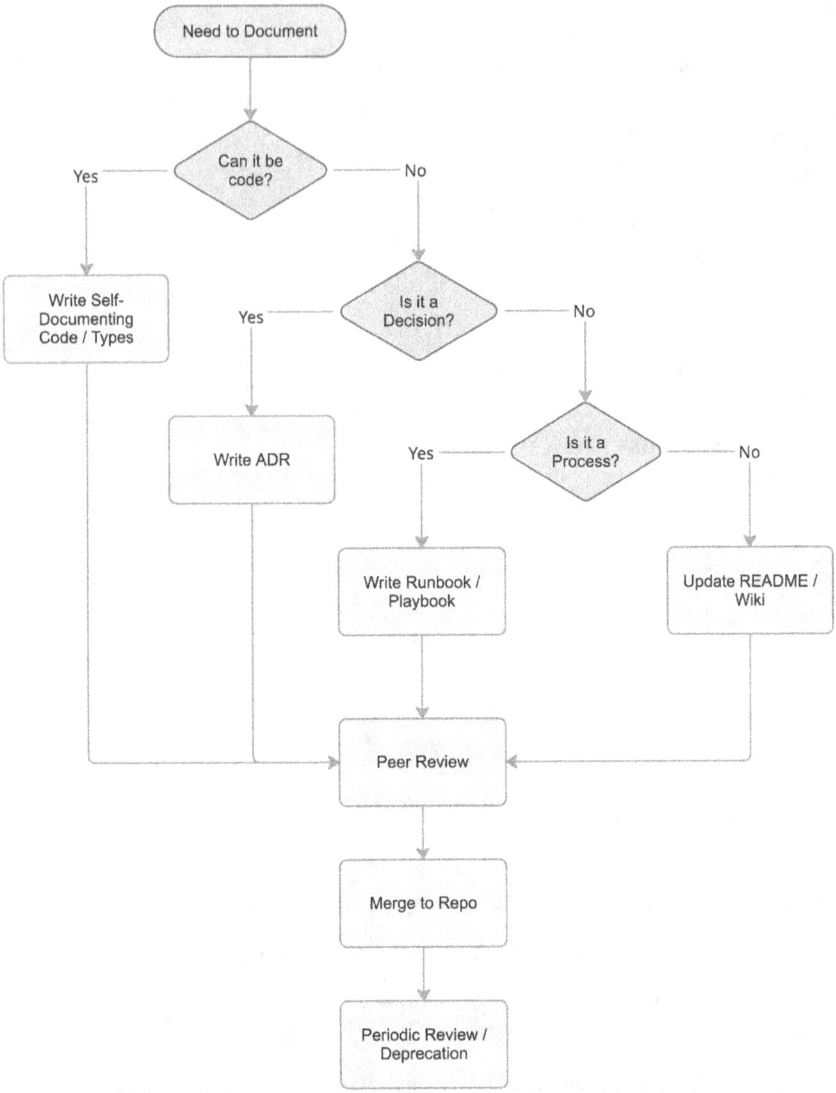

Figure 16.1: Documentation lifecycle – draft, review, publish, maintain; treat documentation as code with versioning and ownership so knowledge stays current and searchable

16.4 Peer Review and Knowledge Sharing

Code review is often misunderstood as a "gatekeeping" process where seniors check juniors' work for mistakes. While quality control is one function, the primary value of code review is **Knowledge Sharing**.

Code review is **asynchronous pair programming** – a mechanism for two (or more) brains to converge on a shared understanding of the system.

The Reviewer's Mindset

When you review code, you are not a teacher grading a test. You are a collaborator.

- **Ask, don't tell.** Instead of "Change this to a map," ask "Did you consider using a map here for faster lookups?"
- **Distinguish between blocking and non-blocking.** Is this a bug (blocking) or a style preference (non-blocking)?
- **Review for clarity, not just correctness.** "I understand what this does, but I had to read it three times" is valid feedback.

The Author's Responsibility

Your Pull Request (PR) is a presentation. You are asking for your teammates' time. Respect it by making your PR easy to review.

Example: A High-Context Pull Request Template

```
### Description

Refactors the payment processing logic to support
↪ multiple currency providers.
```

```
### Why is this change necessary?

We are expanding to the EU market and need to support
↪ Stripe and Adyen.

### Key Changes

-   Introduced `IPaymentProvider` interface.
-   Moved Stripe logic to `StripeProvider` adapter.
-   Added `AdyenProvider` adapter.

### How to Test

1.  Set `PAYMENT_PROVIDER=adyen` in `.env`.
2.  Run `npm test`.
3.  Attempt a checkout flow in the staging
↪   environment.

### Deployment Notes

⚠ Requires the `ADYEN_API_KEY` secret to be set in
↪  the production vault before merging.
```

The Knowledge Sharing Ecosystem

Code review is just one part of the puzzle. A learning culture uses multiple channels to spread knowledge.

A key distinction to make is between **Ephemeral** and **Durable** knowledge.

- **Ephemeral (Chat, Hallway conversations):** Fast and low-friction but lost to time. Good for quick unblocking.
- **Durable (Docs, ADRs, Recorded Talks):** Slower to create but searchable and lasting. Good for architectural decisions and onboarding.

We should constantly strive to move important knowledge from ephemeral channels to durable ones.

16.5 Learning from Failure

> *Regardless of what we discover, we understand and truly believe that everyone did the best job they could, given what they knew at the time, their skills and abilities, the resources available, and the situation at hand.*
>
> — Norm Kerth

16.5.1 Blameless Postmortems

In aviation, when a plane crashes, the NTSB investigates. They don't just blame the pilot; they look at the weather, mechanical systems, training manuals, and communication protocols. They treat the crash as a **system failure**.

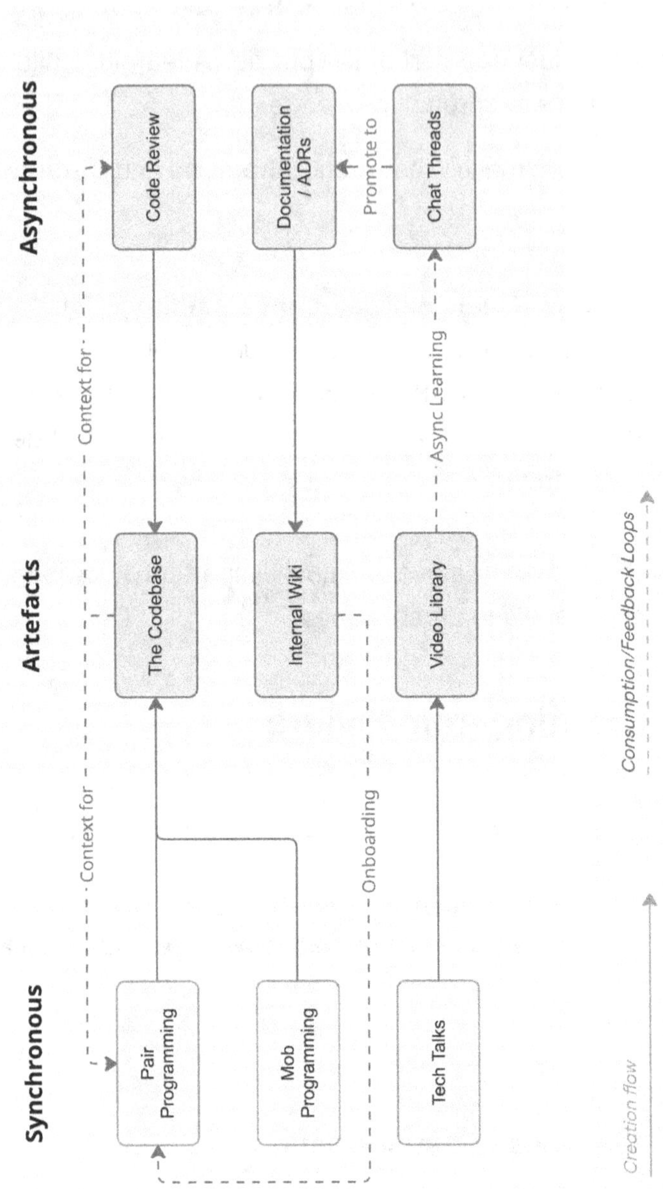

Figure 16.2: Knowledge sharing ecosystem – shift important insights from ephemeral (chat, hallway) to durable (docs, ADRs, recordings) so learning compounds and decisions stay discoverable

In software, we must do the same. When an incident occurs, we conduct a **Blameless Postmortem**.

Why Blameless?

If engineers fear punishment, they will hide mistakes, delete logs, and stay silent when they see a risk. If engineers feel safe, they will say, "I pushed the wrong button because the button was labeled confusingly." That is actionable. We can fix the label, but we cannot "fix" a human to never make mistakes.

16.5.2 Example: Postmortem Template

```
# Incident 2023-11-14: Checkout Service Outage

**Date:** 2023-11-14
**Authors:** Jane Doe, John Smith
**Status:** Resolved
**Impact:**
-   Checkout unavailable for 25 minutes.
-   Estimated 500 failed transactions.

### Timeline

-   **14:00 UTC:** Deployment of v2.3.0 starts.
-   **14:02 UTC:** Alerts fire for "High Error Rate"
↪   on Checkout API.
-   **14:05 UTC:** On-call engineer acknowledges
↪   alert.
-   **14:10 UTC:** Rollback to v2.2.0 initiated.
-   **14:25 UTC:** Service health restored.

### Root Cause Analysis (5 Whys)
```

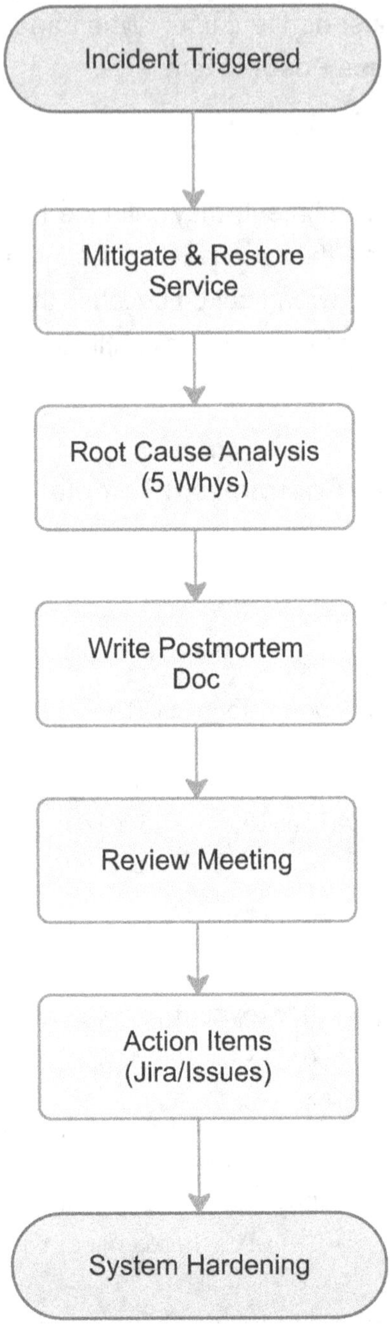

Figure 16.3: Blameless postmortem lifecycle – incident → mitigate → analyze → document → review → actions → hardening; fix systems, not people, so reliability improves

```
1. **Why did the checkout fail?** The database connection pool was exhausted.
2. **Why was the pool exhausted?** The new code opened a connection for every item in the cart instead of one per request.
3. **Why did the code do that?** A loop was refactored, and the connection logic was accidentally moved inside the loop.
4. **Why wasn't this caught in testing?** Our integration tests use a mocked database that doesn't enforce connection limits.
5. **Why don't we test with real limits?** The staging environment configuration drifted from production.

### Action Items

- [ ] **Fix:** Correct the connection logic in the code. (Priority: High)
- [ ] **Process:** Update staging DB config to match production limits. (Priority: Medium)
- [ ] **Tooling:** Add a linter rule to detect database calls inside loops. (Priority: Low)
```

Notice the action items. None of them are "Fire Jane." They are all system fixes: code, configuration, and tooling.

16.6 Conclusion: Culture Eats Process for Breakfast

You can have the best CI/CD pipeline, the cleanest architecture, and 100% test coverage, but if your team hides mistakes, hoards knowledge, and fears collaboration, your software will eventually fail.

Culture is not something that “management” does. **You** create culture every day.

- You create culture when you write a helpful error message.
- You create culture when you thank a reviewer for catching a bug.
- You create culture when you admit, “I broke this, and here is how we can prevent it next time.”

As you grow from a junior engineer to a senior leader, your impact shifts from the code you write to the culture you cultivate. Build a culture where the right thing to do is the easy thing to do.

> Note
>
> **Tools change. Principles don’t.**
> Jira tickets, Slack channels, and GitHub PRs are just tools. The principle is **Shared Understanding**. Use whatever tools help your team understand the system together.

Next, we explore how to amplify this culture with intelligence. *Chapter 17 (AI-Augmented Development Workflows)* examines how to integrate AI agents into your team as collaborative partners, not just tools.

Part VI

The Future of Engineering

Chapter 17:

AI-Augmented Development Workflows

This chapter is a snapshot in time. We are writing this in an era of breathtakingly rapid evolution in Artificial Intelligence. The specific tools, models, and even the job titles that exist today may well be artifacts of the past by the time you read this. It is the only chapter in this book that knowingly runs the risk of becoming outdated.

Why write it? While the tools will change, the principles of collaboration will not. The core pillars of engineering – Lifecycle, Security, Observability, Architecture, and Reliability – do not disappear in the age of AI. They become more important than ever. This chapter is not about learning a specific tool; it's about learning how to partner with a new kind of intelligence to build better systems.

Our goal is to reframe the anxious question, "Will AI take my job?" into a more powerful, strategic one: "How can I leverage AI to do my job better?" The aim is not to code faster, but to think better. AI gives you the leverage to translate high-quality thought into high-quality systems at an unprecedented scale. Let's explore how.

17.1 Your Newest Teammate: The AI Co-Engineer

Think of the relationship between a senior airline pilot and a modern flight computer. The pilot provides the high-level intent – the destination, the route, the strategy for navigating a storm. They are responsible for the safety and success of the entire journey. The flight computer executes thousands of micro-adjustments per second, manages complex subsystems, and handles routine tasks with relentless precision. The computer does not replace the pilot's judgment; it amplifies it.

This is the mental model for your collaboration with AI. You are the pilot. The AI is your co-engineer, a tireless intern, and a Socratic partner all rolled into one. It can write boilerplate code in seconds, recall obscure API details instantly, and check your work for common errors without getting tired or bored.

Your role shifts from being the primary writer of syntax to being the primary director of semantics – the meaning and intent behind the code. This is where the practice of Prompt Engineering becomes less about magic words and more about clear, technical direction.

> **Note**
>
> Effective prompt engineering is simply clear communication. It's the art of providing an AI with the same context, constraints, and success criteria you would give a human junior engineer.

Consider the difference. A vague request leads to a vague and likely flawed result. A precise, context-aware request leads to a robust, high-quality outcome.

Example: Vague vs. Directed Prompts

Imagine you ask an AI: "Create a function to add a user to the database." The AI, lacking context, might produce something simplistic and insecure.

Now, consider a more professional prompt: *"Create a TypeScript function for a NestJS service that adds a new user. Use the repository pattern with TypeORM. The function should accept a* `CreateUserDto`*. Hash the password with* `bcrypt` *before saving. Handle potential duplicate email errors (PostgreSQL unique constraint violation) by throwing a NestJS* `ConflictException`*. Return a* `User` *entity, but ensure the password field is excluded from the final DTO returned to the client."*

This is not just a prompt; it's a micro-specification. The quality of the AI's output is a direct reflection of the quality of your input.

```
// An example of code generated from a well-crafted,
↪  specific prompt.
import { ConflictException, Injectable } from
↪  '@nestjs/common';
import { InjectRepository } from '@nestjs/typeorm';
import { Repository } from 'typeorm';
import * as bcrypt from 'bcrypt';
import { User } from './user.entity';
import { CreateUserDto } from './dto/create-user.dto';

@Injectable()
export class UsersService {
  constructor(
    @InjectRepository(User)
    private usersRepository: Repository<User>,
  ) {}
```

```
  async create(createUserDto: CreateUserDto):
  ↪  Promise<Omit<User, 'password'>> {
    // Intent: Hash the password before storing it.
    const salt = await bcrypt.genSalt();
    const hashedPassword = await
    ↪  bcrypt.hash(createUserDto.password, salt);

    const user = this.usersRepository.create({
      ...createUserDto,
      password: hashedPassword,
    });

    try {
      const newUser = await
      ↪  this.usersRepository.save(user);
      // Intent: Never return the password hash.
      const { password, ...result } = newUser;
      return result;
    } catch (error) {
      // Intent: Handle specific database errors
      ↪  gracefully.
      if (error.code === '23505') { // PostgreSQL
      ↪  unique violation
        throw new ConflictException('Email already
        ↪  exists');
      }
      throw error;
    }
  }
}
```

17.2 The Rise of Autonomous Agents

The next step in this evolution moves beyond interactive copilots to delegable agents. If a copilot is your pair programmer, an agent is the junior engineer you can assign a complete, well-defined task to. This is like an architect handing a detailed blueprint to a team of hyper-efficient robotic builders. The architect's value is in the quality and clarity of the blueprint, not in laying the bricks.

These agents can take a high-level goal, break it down into steps, and execute them. A single prompt like, *"Implement the password reset feature defined in ticket JIRA-123. Use our standard API patterns, ensure 100% test coverage for the new services, and open a pull request assigned to me,"* is rapidly moving from science fiction to reality.

This transforms the entire development workflow. The engineer becomes the director and validator in a highly automated system.

In this workflow, the engineer's most critical contributions happen at the beginning (defining the "what" and "why") and at the end (validating the final result against that intent). The "how" becomes increasingly automated. This represents a transformation in development workflow.

17.3 The New Mandate: Director and Validator

When your collaborator can generate a thousand lines of code in the time it takes you to read a single function, your value fundamentally shifts. It no longer comes from the volume of code you can personally write. It comes from your ability to:

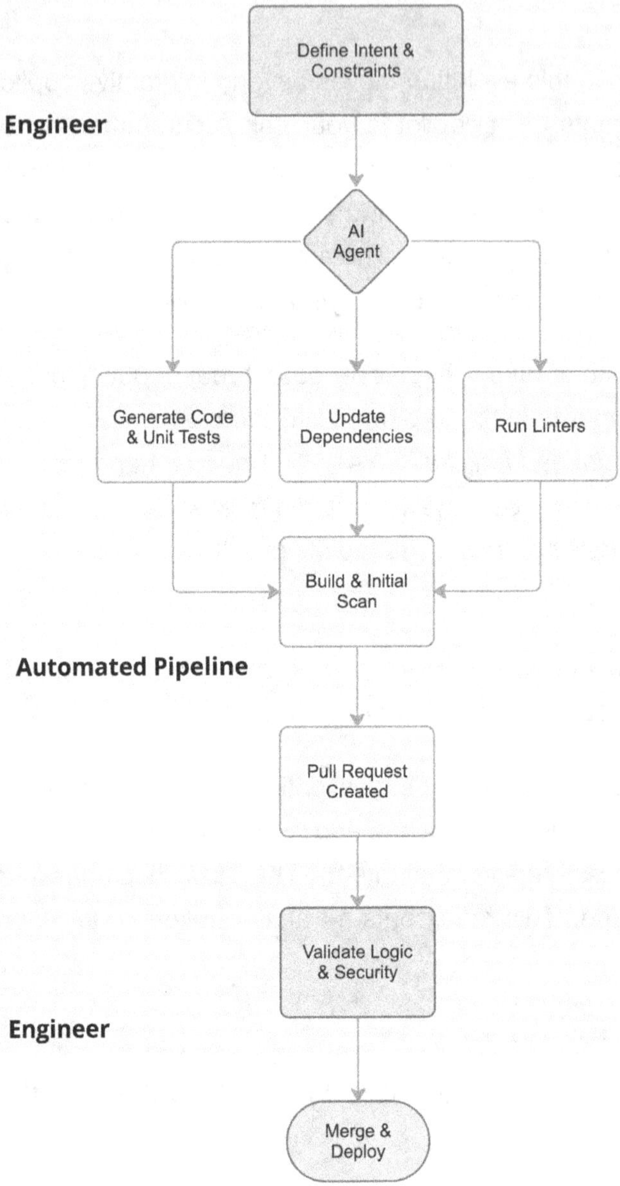

Figure 17.1: AI-augmented workflow – engineer sets intent and criteria; agents decompose, generate code and tests, open PRs; human validates outcomes against business and quality gates

1. **Reason about systems:** Decompose a complex problem into small, well-defined tasks that an agent can execute.
2. **Manage trade-offs:** Make the difficult architectural decisions that AI cannot.
3. **Ask the right questions:** Interrogate the system, challenge assumptions, and design experiments to reveal hidden flaws.
4. **Validate outcomes:** Prove that the AI's output is not just syntactically correct, but logically sound, secure, reliable, and aligned with the business goal.

This final point – validation – is the bedrock of the new engineering mandate. An AI can be a brilliant refactoring engine, but it lacks the domain context to know if the refactored code preserves a subtle but critical business rule.

Example: The Human Validation Step

Imagine you task an AI with refactoring a legacy function.

```
# A legacy function with some unclear logic.
def calculate_shipping_cost(items, user_country,
↪ user_status):
    cost = 0
    # ... 50 lines of complex, nested conditional
    ↪ logic ...
    # A magic number that was added years ago to
    ↪ handle a specific partner's VAT.
    if user_country == "DE" and user_status ==
    ↪ "premium_plus":
        cost = cost * 0.85
    return cost
```

You could ask an AI: *"Refactor this function to be more readable and add unit tests."* The AI will likely do an excellent job of simplifying the structure and generating comprehensive tests for the logic it can see. However, it has no way of understanding the *unwritten context* of that magic number, `0.85`.

It might correctly test that for a German premium-plus user, the discount is 15%. But your job as the human validator is to ask the deeper question: *"Is this 15% discount still correct? Or was it a temporary promotion that should have been removed years ago?"* The AI optimizes the code; you validate the business logic.

AI doesn't replace engineering thinking – it makes the quality of your thinking more visible. A bug in AI-generated code is often a bug in the prompt, a flaw in the specification, or a failure of validation.

As we move toward a world where systems can write themselves, our primary responsibility becomes ensuring they write the *right* system. But how do you cultivate the judgment to do that? The answer lies not in mastering the tools, but in mastering the thinking that directs them. In *Chapter 18 (From Tools to Thinking)*, we will explore how to build the deep mental models that allow you to remain the architect, not just the operator, in this new era.

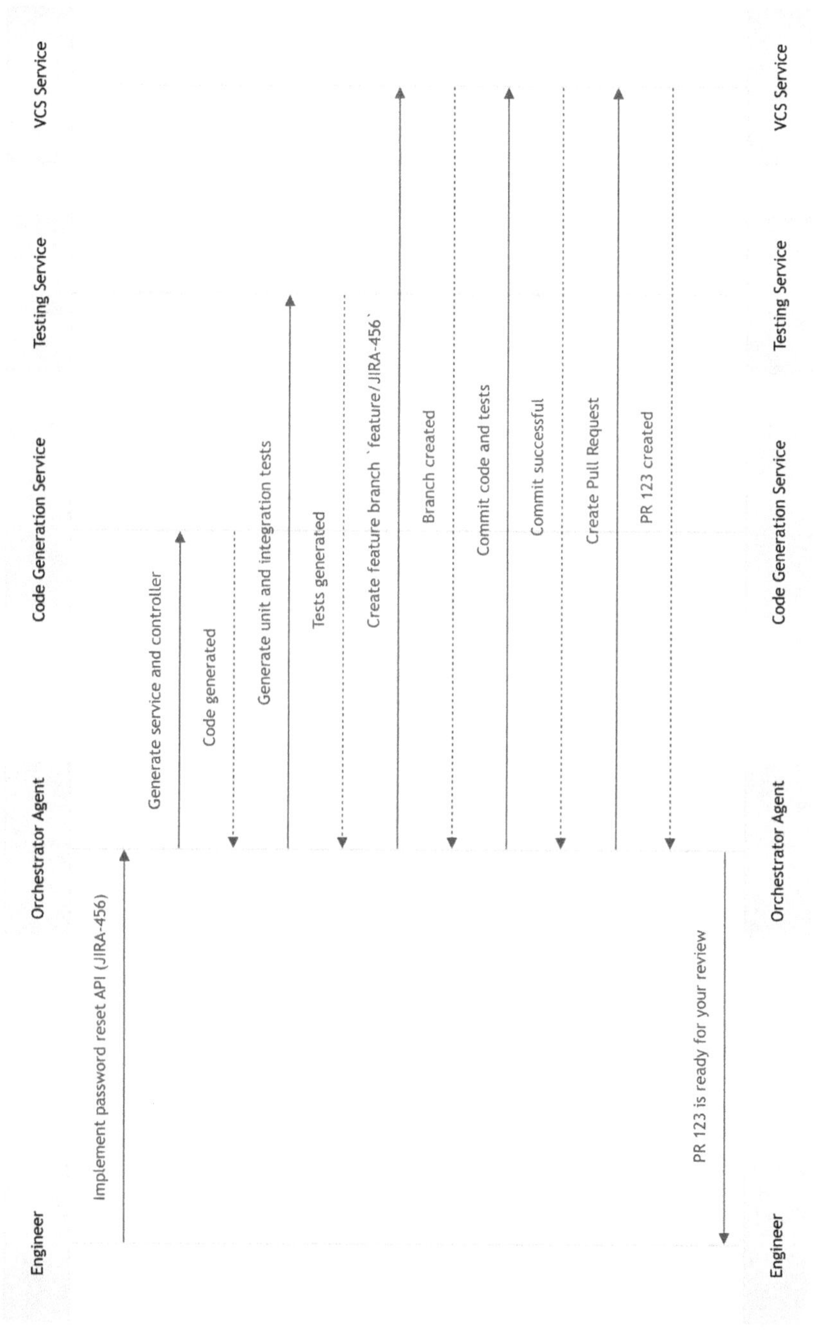

Figure 17.2: Human validation step – AI can refactor and test, but engineers verify domain rules, edge cases, and trade-offs to ensure the right system is built

Chapter 18:

From Tools to Thinking

The factory of the future will have only two employees, a man and a dog. The man will be there to feed the dog. The dog will be there to keep the man from touching the equipment.
— Warren Bennis

For decades, the software industry has conflated "coding" with "engineering." We measured value by lines of code, commit frequency, and the ability to recall obscure syntax from memory. If you could type C++ pointer arithmetic without segfaulting[1], you were an engineer.

That era is over.

Generative AI has commoditized syntax. It can write the boilerplate, the unit tests, the documentation, and even the complex algorithms faster than you can type `def`. For many junior engineers, this feels

[1]Triggering a **segmentation fault** – a fatal runtime error raised by the operating system when a program attempts to access memory outside the bounds of its permitted address space. In C and C++, this most commonly results from incorrect pointer arithmetic, dereferencing invalid or freed pointers, or out-of-bounds memory access. The term is often used informally to denote a catastrophic crash caused by low-level memory misuse.

like an existential threat. If the machine can code, what is left for the human?

The answer is everything that matters.

The "End of Coding" is actually the **Beginning of Engineering**. As the mechanical act of writing text becomes automated, the value shifts to the higher-order skills we discussed in *Chapter 4 (From Coder to System Thinker)*: systems thinking, architectural design, and the ability to frame problems so precisely that a machine cannot misunderstand them.

18.1 The Commodity of Syntax

Consider the transition from manual calculation to spreadsheets in the 1980s. Before VisiCalc and Excel, "computers" were often humans who performed arithmetic all day. When spreadsheets arrived, the job of "doing the math" disappeared overnight.

But accountants didn't disappear. They evolved into financial analysts.

Freed from the drudgery of manual addition, they could focus on *modeling* the business, testing hypotheses ("What if revenue drops 10%?"), and interpreting the results. The tool didn't replace them; it elevated them from arithmetic to analysis.

We are at a similar inflection point. **Syntax Generation** – the act of typing valid code – is becoming a commodity.

In this new world, "working code" is the baseline, not the goal. The bottleneck shifts from *production* to *verification* and *comprehension*. The question is no longer "Can you write this function?" but "Should this function exist, and do you understand what it does?"

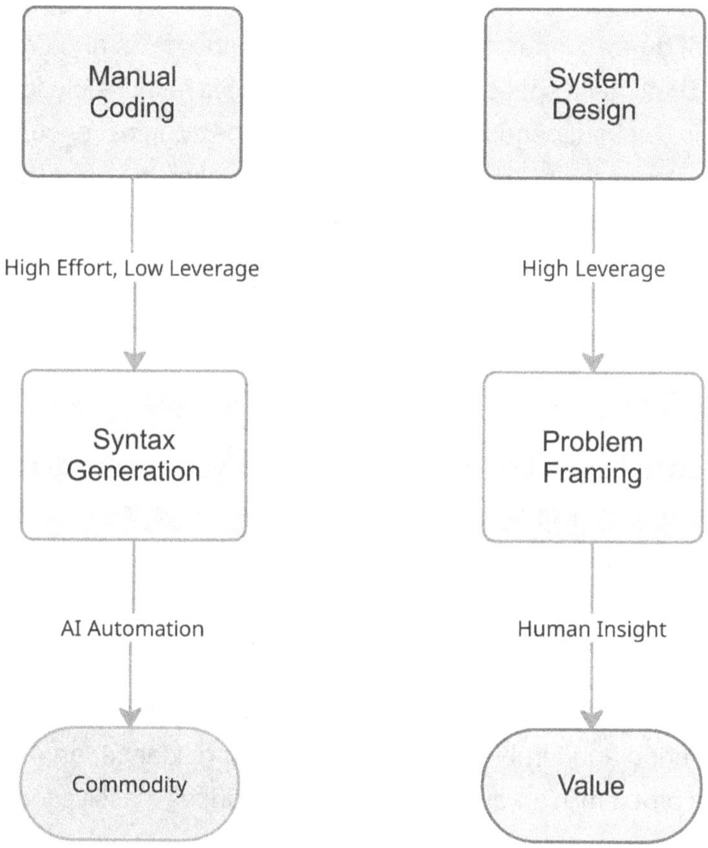

Figure 18.1: From syntax to thinking – tools commoditize code generation; value shifts to modeling, verification, and comprehension across the engineering workflow

18.2 The Editor-in-Chief Mindset

If you are no longer the primary writer of code, what are you?

You are the **Editor-in-Chief**.

Think of a newspaper. Reporters (the AI) gather facts and draft stories at breakneck speed. But the Editor (you) is responsible for what goes on the front page. The Editor checks the sources, ensures the tone matches the publication's standards, verifies the facts, and decides if the story is relevant to the readers.

In an AI-augmented workflow, your role evolves from "Debugging" to "Auditing."

> ⚠ Warning
>
> You are responsible for every line of code you commit, regardless of who – or what – wrote it. "The AI wrote it" is never a valid excuse for a production outage.

Example: The "Correct" but "Wrong" Solution

AI models are trained on the internet, which contains both brilliant engineering and terrible hacks. Without your guidance, an AI might solve a problem in a way that works but introduces massive technical debt.

Consider a request to parse a date string in Python.

```
# The AI might generate this "working" code
# Intent: Parse a date string like "2023-10-27"
def parse_date_manual(date_str):
    # ⚠ Intent Comment: This reinvents the wheel and
    ↪ is fragile
```

```
    parts = date_str.split('-')
    if len(parts) != 3:
        return None
    return {"year": int(parts[0]), "month":
    ↪  int(parts[1]), "day": int(parts[2])}

# The Engineer (You) knows the standard library is
↪  safer
from datetime import datetime

def parse_date_correct(date_str):
    # ✅ Intent Comment: Uses standard library for
    ↪  robustness and timezone support
    return datetime.strptime(date_str, "%Y-%m-%d")
```

The first function works. It passes tests. But it ignores leap years, timezones, and validation. An AI might offer it because it saw similar code in a beginner's tutorial. The **Editor-in-Chief** rejects it in favor of the robust, standard approach.

18.3 Problem Framing is the New Syntax

If syntax is cheap, **Problem Framing** is expensive.

Working with AI is like making a wish to a Genie in a lamp. You get *exactly* what you ask for, which is often dangerous if you ask vaguely. If you ask for "a fast way to sort numbers," the Genie might give you a sorting algorithm that consumes all your memory.

The primary creative act of the future engineer is **Specification**. You must define the constraints, the inputs, the outputs, and the edge cases so clearly that the implementation becomes inevitable.

Example: Intent vs. Implementation

In TypeScript, we can use types to define the “shape of the truth” before we write a single line of logic. This is “Prompt as Code.”

```
import { z } from 'zod';

// The Engineer defines the INTENT (The "What")
// We want a user profile, but age must be realistic,
↪ and email valid.
const UserProfileSchema = z.object({
  username: z.string().min(3),
  email: z.string().email(),
  age: z.number().min(13).max(120), // Constraint: No
↪ toddlers or immortals
  role: z.enum(['admin', 'user', 'guest'])
});

type UserProfile = z.infer<typeof UserProfileSchema>;

// The AI implements the LOGIC (The "How") based on
↪ your constraints
function validateAndCreateUser(input: unknown):
↪ UserProfile {
  // Intent: Validate input against the strict schema
  ↪ defined above
  const result = UserProfileSchema.safeParse(input);

  if (!result.success) {
    throw new Error(`Invalid user data:
    ↪ ${result.error.message}`);
  }

  return result.data;
}
```

Here, you didn't write the validation logic (the `if` statements). You defined the *schema*. You framed the problem. The AI (or the library) handled the mechanics.

18.4 The AI Verification Loop

This shift changes our development lifecycle. It moves from a linear "Write -> Test -> Deploy" to a circular "Frame -> Generate -> Verify" loop.

Your value is applied at the beginning (Framing) and the end (Review). The middle is where the machine lives.

18.5 Conclusion: The Renaissance of Engineering

Do not fear the end of coding. Embrace it.

When you don't have to spend four hours debugging a missing semicolon, you have four hours to think about data consistency. When you don't have to write boilerplate CRUD endpoints, you can focus on the security architecture of your API.

We are entering a Renaissance of Engineering. We are being freed from the assembly line of syntax to return to the true craft: designing systems that solve human problems.

The tools have changed. The principles – clarity, reliability, security, and responsibility – remain exactly the same.

With this new mindset, your focus shifts from immediate tasks to long-term impact. In the next chapter, *Chapter 19 (Legacy and Men-*

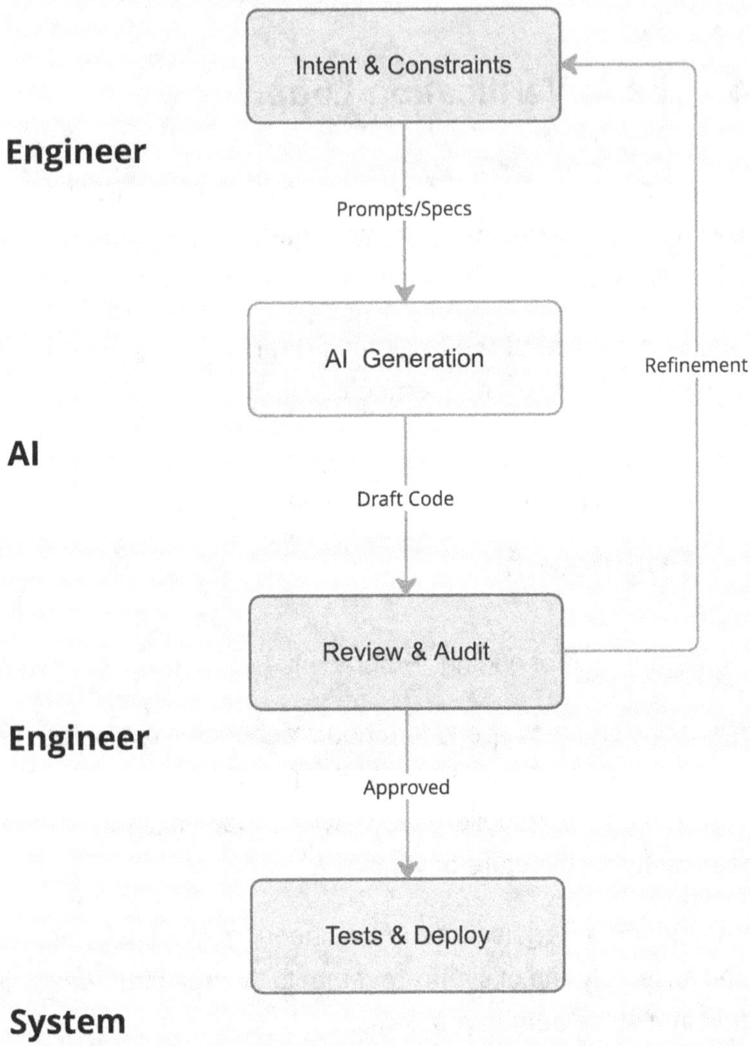

Figure 18.2: AI verification loop – Frame intent and constraints → Generate drafts → Human review and audit → Tests and deploy; tighten the spec each cycle

torship), we will explore how to translate this engineering wisdom into a lasting career and guide the next generation.

Chapter 19:

Legacy and Mentorship

The true meaning of life is to plant trees, under whose shade you do not expect to sit.
— Nelson Henderson

If you are reading this, you have likely spent years mastering the craft of code. You understand the pillars of engineering, you can architect complex systems, and you know how to collaborate with AI. But there is one final frontier that separates a senior engineer from a true leader: **Legacy**.

In software engineering, "legacy" is often a dirty word. It conjures images of spaghetti code, outdated frameworks, and "here be dragons" comments. But let's reframe that. **Legacy code is simply code that has been successful enough to survive.**

Your goal as an engineer is not just to write code that works today. It is to build systems – and teams – that thrive long after you have moved on. This chapter is about the responsibility of stewardship, the art of mentorship, and how to ensure your work outlives your tenure.

19.1 The "Bus Factor" Reality Check

Imagine a critical service in your infrastructure. It processes payments, or perhaps it handles user authentication. It runs on a server that sits metaphorically (or sometimes literally) in a kitchen. It hasn't been redeployed in two years.

Why? Because the only person who understood how it worked left the company 18 months ago.

This is the **"Ghost System."** It is a terrifying liability. The team lives in fear of the day it crashes, because no one knows how to fix it.

This scenario highlights the **Bus Factor**: the minimum number of team members that have to be suddenly lost (e.g., "hit by a bus," though we prefer "won the lottery") before the project stalls due to lack of knowledge.

If your Bus Factor is 1 – if *you* are the only person who understands a critical system – you are not an asset to your company. You are a single point of failure.

Designing for the Future

Building for legacy means designing systems that are discoverable and maintainable by people who have never met you. It means accepting a humble truth: **The primary maintainer of your code in six months will likely be someone else (or you, having forgotten everything).**

Code as Communication

We often say "code is for humans first, computers second." When you write code with legacy in mind, you are writing a letter to the future. This principle is central to code readability.

Consider this "clever" Python snippet:

```
# BAD: Clever, concise, but opaque
def p(d):
    return [x for x in d if x['s'] == 'A' and x['v'] >
    ↪  100]
```

It works. It's fast. But it requires the reader to hold the entire context in their head. Now, look at the "legacy-ready" version:

```
# GOOD: Explicit, typed, and self-documenting
from typing import List, Dict, Any

def filter_high_value_active_orders(orders:
↪  List[Dict[str, Any]]) -> List[Dict[str, Any]]:
    """
    Filters orders to return only those that are
↪   Active ('A')
    and have a value greater than $100.

    Why: These are the only orders eligible for the
↪   'Gold' processing tier.
    See Design Doc:
↪   https://<internal>.wiki/design/gold-tier-processing
    """
    ACTIVE_STATUS = 'A'
    HIGH_VALUE_THRESHOLD = 100

    return [
        order for order in orders
        if order['status'] == ACTIVE_STATUS
        and order['value'] > HIGH_VALUE_THRESHOLD
    ]
```

The second version is longer. It takes more time to type. But it answers the questions the future maintainer will have: *What does this do? Why does it do it? Where is the documentation?* This is self-documenting code.

Documentation as a Love Letter

Documentation is often the first casualty of a deadline. But in the context of legacy, documentation is the bridge between your intent and the future reality.

You don't need to document every line. You need to document the **decisions**.

- **Why** did we choose this architecture?
- **Why** are we using this specific library version?
- **What** alternatives did we reject, and why?

Use "Why" comments to capture context that cannot be expressed in code.

```
// BAD: Just the fix
// Fix for issue #452
const timeout = 5000;

// GOOD: The Context
// WORKAROUND: The external payment gateway has a
↪  known race condition
// where it drops connections if the handshake takes <
↪  100ms.
// We introduce a synthetic delay to ensure stability.
// Tracking issue for vendor fix:
↪  https://<vendor>.com/issues/992
// TODO: Remove this delay once vendor releases v2.1
↪  (expected Q4 2025)
const MIN_HANDSHAKE_DELAY_MS = 100;
```

19.2 Mentorship as an Engineering Discipline

If building maintainable code is about preserving the *system*, mentorship is about preserving the *culture* and *capability*.

In traditional craftsmanship – blacksmithing, carpentry, stonemasonry – you were not considered a Master until you had successfully trained an Apprentice. The same should be true for software engineering.

Seniority is not measured by how much code you write. It is measured by how many other engineers you enable.

19.2.1 The Virtuous Cycle of Teaching

Mentorship is not a charity. It is a selfish act of engineering optimization.

1. **It scales your impact.** You can only write so much code. If you teach five people to write code as well as you, your impact is multiplied by five.
2. **It solidifies your knowledge.** You never truly understand a concept until you have to explain it to a beginner (the Feynman Technique).
3. **It builds resilience.** The more people who understand the system, the higher the Bus Factor, and the better you sleep at night.

19.2.2 Code Reviews as Mentorship

The most frequent mentorship opportunity is the Pull Request (PR). Code review also serves as a teaching tool.

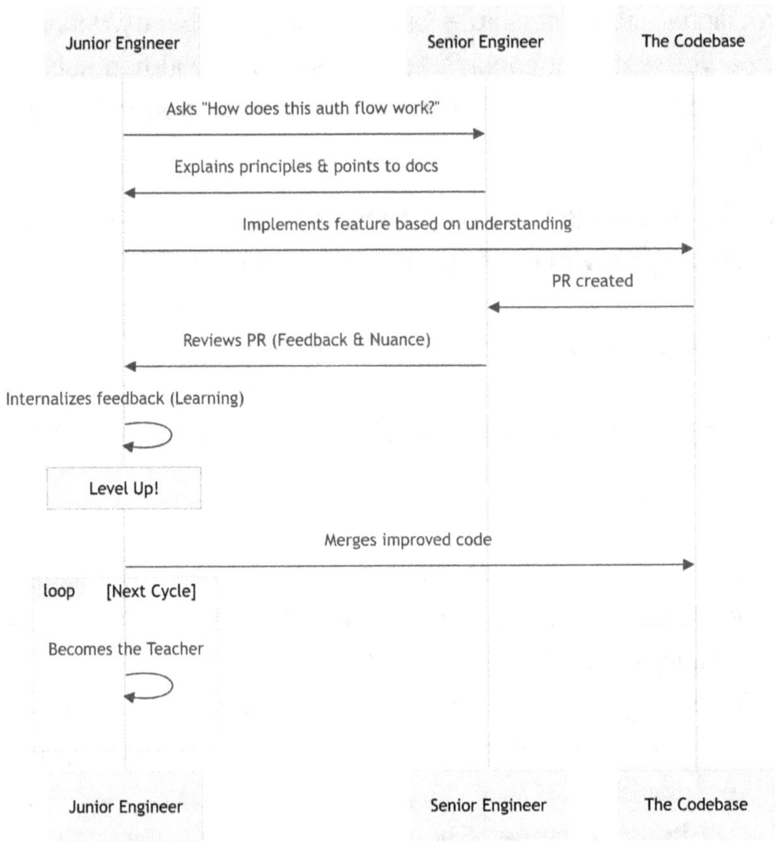

Figure 19.1: Mentorship virtuous cycle – teaching multiplies impact, deepens understanding, and raises the Bus Factor so teams stay resilient when individuals move on

Don't just look for bugs. Look for **teaching moments**.

- Instead of saying "Change this to X," ask "What happens if we receive a null value here?"
- Instead of rewriting the code yourself, explain the pattern that would solve the problem elegantly.
- Praise good work explicitly. "I really like how you handled the error case here – very robust."

A code review is a dialogue, not a gatekeeping exercise.

19.3 From Implicit to Explicit Knowledge

One of the biggest challenges in legacy planning is moving knowledge out of your head (Implicit) and into the system (Explicit).

- **Implicit:** "Oh, yeah, you have to restart the service if the queue gets stuck. Dave knows how to do it."
- **Explicit (Docs):** A runbook entry titled "Troubleshooting: Stuck Queue" with step-by-step instructions.
- **Executable (Code/Tests):** A script that detects a stuck queue and restarts the service automatically, or a test that prevents the queue from getting stuck in the first place.

Your goal should always be to move knowledge to the right: from Head $\rightarrow$ Docs $\rightarrow$ Code. This process enables knowledge sharing across the team.

19.4 Conclusion: The Torch Pass

As we conclude this book, I want you to think about your career not as a series of jobs, but as a body of work.

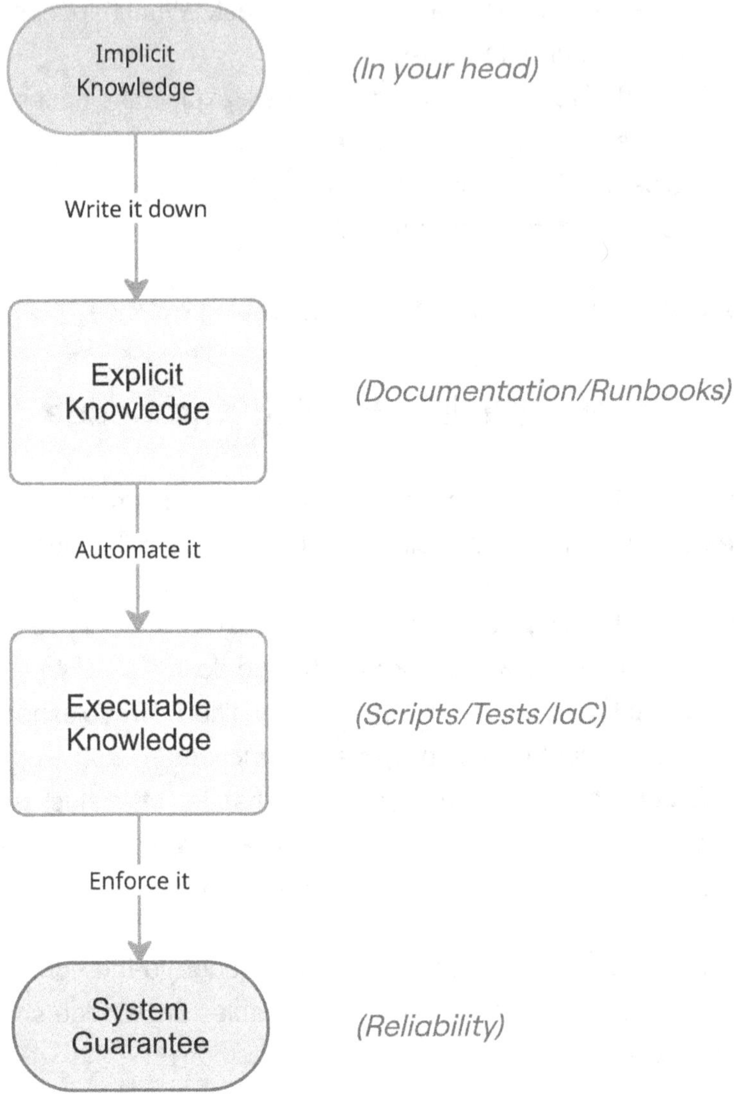

Figure 19.2: From implicit to explicit knowledge – write it down (docs), then automate (scripts/tests) until the system guarantees reliability without tribal memory

The systems you build will eventually be replaced. The code you write will be refactored or deleted. That is the nature of our industry.

But the **principles** you instill in your code – clarity, robustness, honesty – and the **skills** you pass on to the engineers around you… those things endure.

Your true legacy is not the code that runs on the server. It is the team that can keep running it without you.

Build systems that last. Teach others to do the same. And when the time comes, pass the torch with confidence, knowing you have left the campsite better than you found it.

This final act of mentorship completes the journey we began in this book. You have evolved from a coder into a system thinker, armed with the foundational pillars of modern engineering. You have learned that our craft is a discipline of clarity, structure, and responsibility. The future is not just about collaborating with AI, but about using these timeless principles to build systems – and people – that last.

> Tip
>
> **Final Thought:**
> *Engineering is not about being the smartest person in the room. It is about making the room smarter.*

Part VII

Appendices

Chapter 20:

Ten Author's Recommendations to Aspiring Software Engineers

Software engineering is a journey that often feels like navigating a labyrinth. It is technically demanding, intellectually rigorous, and socially complex. While code is the medium we work in, the actual job is about solving problems, managing complexity, and collaborating with humans.

This appendix steps away from code samples and diagrams. It offers ten of the author's recommendations, drawn from experience and meant to serve as anchors when the path feels confusing. They are not rules but compasses you can return to throughout your career, turning the book's pillars into everyday habits.

1. The Terminal is Your Friend

The graphical user interface (GUI) is a comfortable blanket, but the Command Line Interface (CLI) is a power tool. The earlier you make peace with it, the better.

Think of the terminal as the cockpit instruments in a plane. The glossy screens are nice, but it is the direct controls that show you how things really work. GUIs are excellent for making easy tasks intuitive, but they often hide the complexity you need to understand to become an expert. The terminal lets you chain commands, automate tedious workflows, and interact with the operating system at a deeper level. Whether it is Git, server management, or build tools, fluency in the terminal often separates a junior developer from a senior engineer.

2. Find Your Mentor

Growth is rarely a solitary endeavor. You need a good mentor who can show you the path and illuminate it.

Imagine hiking an unfamiliar mountain alone with a tourist map versus walking it with a local guide. The map might eventually get you there, but the guide saves you from dead ends, bad weather, and dangerous shortcuts. A mentor is not just someone who corrects your code. They also help correct your course. They can help you distinguish between hype and value, navigate office politics, and spot pitfalls that you, due to limited experience, cannot yet see. Do not wait for a mentor to be assigned to you. Seek one out actively and invest in the relationship.

3. Learn English

This recommendation may sound strange because if you are reading this, you are likely already on the safe side. However, it cannot be overstated: **English is the lingua franca of technology.**

The best documentation, the richest developer communities, and many cutting-edge tutorials are written in English. Increasingly, the most capable AI tools you use – code assistants, search copilots, and chat-based helpers – also work best when you can express your questions clearly in English. It is the default language of the global engineering conversation. If you want full access to the global repository of knowledge, you must be comfortable reading and writing in the language of the web. Improving your English is not about sounding fancy; instead, it is about widening the pipe through which you learn and collaborate.

4. The Aim is Not to Code Faster, but to Think Better

Be a software engineer, not just a coder.

Typing speed is almost never the bottleneck in software development. The real bottleneck is understanding the problem. An engineer spends most of their time reading, designing, and thinking, and only a minority of it typing. If you rush to code without a plan, you build technical debt, not solutions. Like a good chess player, you win not by moving pieces faster but by seeing patterns and thinking several moves ahead.

> **Note**
>
> A "Coder" implements what they are told. An "Engineer" questions the requirements, considers edge cases, and designs for scalability.

5. Serve as Attorney for Your Solutions

You must advocate for your technical decisions, but you must do so with grace. Serve as an attorney for yourself to "sell" your solutions, but be fair and respectful about others' solutions and decisions.

Software engineering is a team sport. You will disagree with colleagues about architecture, style, and priorities. When you do, think like a calm lawyer presenting a case, not a debater trying to win at all costs.

- Argue based on trade-offs, not personal preferences.
- Remember that in most situations there is more than one reasonable option.
- Recognize that there is rarely a single "right" solution, only the solution that best fits the current constraints.

Your goal is not to prove that you are right, but to help the team converge on a decision they understand and can support.

6. Master the Fundamentals; Frameworks are Just Fashion

Do not tie your identity to a specific framework or library (for example, "I am a React developer"). Frameworks change every few years; the underlying principles do not.

Think of frameworks as outfits and fundamentals as your skeleton and muscles. Outfits change with seasons and taste; the underlying structure stays. Focus your energy on understanding data structures, algorithms, design patterns, and how the Internet works (HTTP, DNS, databases). If you understand the underlying principles of how a hash map works or how a browser renders a page, picking up the "hot new framework" will take you a weekend rather than a month. The best code you read in the wild is usually just these fundamentals expressed clearly.

7. Read Code Like a Writer Reads Books

One of the best ways to see these fundamentals in action is to study good code.

Aspiring authors read the classics to understand style, structure, and narrative. Aspiring engineers must do the same.

You will spend significantly more time reading code (often legacy code written by someone who has already left the company) than writing new code. Treat reading code as a skill you can practice. Browse open-source repositories on GitHub. Study how experienced developers structure their projects, name their variables, and handle errors. Notice what makes certain code feel calm and understandable, and what makes other code feel chaotic. You cannot write clean code if you have never seen what clean code looks like.

8. Understand the Business "Why"

You are not paid to write code; you are paid to solve business problems using code.

The most valuable engineers understand the domain they are working in, whether it is finance, healthcare, or e-commerce. Before you write a single line, ask: *What value does this feature add? Is this the most efficient way to solve the user's problem?* Sometimes, the best code is no code at all because you realize the feature is unnecessary or the problem can be solved with a simpler change to process or configuration.

Understanding the business context makes your technical decisions sharper. It helps you prioritize, negotiate scope, and suggest alternatives that create more value with less effort.

9. Don't Reinvent the Wheel

There is a time for academic curiosity, and there is a time for shipping products. Learn to distinguish between the two.

If a robust, well-maintained library exists to solve a standard problem (like date formatting, authentication, or mathematical calculations), use it. Your custom implementation will likely be less secure, more buggy, and harder to maintain than the community-standard solution. Reinvention has its place when you are learning or exploring, but in production systems, humility often means standing on the shoulders of giants.

10. Treat Your Health as a Critical Dependency

Software engineering is a marathon, not a sprint. Burnout is a real and dangerous threat in our industry.

Treat yourself like production infrastructure: you need monitoring, capacity planning, and maintenance. You cannot think clearly or solve complex logic puzzles if you are sleep-deprived and fueled only by caffeine. Your brain is your hardware; if you do not maintain it with sleep, movement, and time away from the screen, your performance will degrade. To be a long-term productive engineer, you must cultivate a life outside of the terminal.

Make rest, relationships, and non-technical interests part of your career strategy, not an afterthought. A sustainable engineering career is built on a healthy human being.

These ten recommendations are not a checklist you complete once and forget. They are habits and perspectives you revisit as your responsibilities grow and your context changes. As you move through your career, come back to this list occasionally and ask yourself: which of these do I want to strengthen next?

Chapter 21:

Glossary

This glossary anchors the book's vocabulary so you can move fast without ambiguity. Each entry favors principle over tooling, links to its first use, and ties back to the core pillars. Use it as a quick reference when a term feels familiar but the intent needs precision.

5 Whys

An iterative interrogative technique used to explore the cause-and-effect relationships underlying a particular problem to determine the root cause.

Example usage: Appears in *Chapter 16 (Pillar 7 – Collaboration and Culture)* (context: root cause analysis)

Related pillars: Collaboration | Reliability

ADR (Architecture Decision Record)

A document capturing an important architectural decision, its context, and its consequences to preserve the "why" behind the choice.

Example usage: Appears in *Chapter 13 (Pillar 4 – Architecture and Design)* (context: documenting trade-offs)

Related pillars: Architecture | Collaboration

Agentic AI

AI systems capable of autonomous action and decision-making within defined boundaries, acting as collaborators in software development rather than passive code generators.

Example usage: Appears in *Chapter 3 (The AI-Augmented Era: Tools Change, Principles Don't)* (context: transformation of development workflow)

Related pillars: Lifecycle

Architecture

The continuous process of making decisions that are hard to change later; focuses on structure, boundaries, and trade-offs.

Example usage: Appears in *Chapter 13 (Pillar 4 – Architecture and Design)* (context: definition of architecture)

Related pillars: Architecture

Artifact

An immutable, versioned package (binary, container, or zip) produced by the build process that is ready to be deployed to any environment.

Example usage: Appears in *Chapter 10 (Pillar 1 – Lifecycle Management)* (context: build once, deploy many)

Related pillars: Lifecycle | Security

Backoff

An algorithm that increases the delay between retries of a failed operation (often exponentially) to prevent overwhelming a struggling dependency.

Example usage: Appears in *Chapter 14 (Pillar 5 – Reliability and Resilience)* (context: retry strategies)

Related pillars: Reliability

Big Ball of Mud

A sprawling, ad-hoc system with weak boundaries and pervasive coupling, grown without coherent architecture or discipline.

Example usage: Appears in *Chapter 13 (Pillar 4 – Architecture and Design)* (context: modularity motivation)

Related pillars: Architecture | Reliability

Black Box Risk

The danger of using AI-generated code without understanding its logic, leaving engineers unable to debug or adapt when tools fail or produce incorrect results.

Example usage: Appears in *Chapter 3 (The AI-Augmented Era: Tools Change, Principles Don't)* (context: warning about accepting AI output without verification)

Related pillars: All pillars (foundational concept)

Blameless Postmortem

An incident analysis process focused on identifying systemic causes rather than blaming individuals, fostering a culture where it is safe to learn from failure.

Example usage: Appears in *Chapter 16 (Pillar 7 – Collaboration and Culture)* (context: learning from failure)

Related pillars: Collaboration | Reliability

Blue-Green Deployment

A release strategy using two identical environments where one is live (Blue) and the other (Green) is updated, allowing instant switch-over.

Example usage: Appears in *Chapter 10 (Pillar 1 – Lifecycle Management)* (context: zero-downtime releases)

Related pillars: Lifecycle | Reliability

Bounded Context

A specific boundary within a domain where a particular model and language apply, preventing ambiguity (e.g., “Customer” in Sales vs. Support).

Example usage: Appears in *Chapter 13 (Pillar 4 – Architecture and Design)* (context: Domain-Driven Design)

Related pillars: Architecture

Bulkhead

A pattern that isolates elements of an application into pools so that if one fails, the others will continue to function (like watertight compartments in a ship).

Example usage: Appears in *Chapter 14 (Pillar 5 – Reliability and Resilience)* (context: resource isolation)

Related pillars: Reliability | Architecture

Bus Factor

The minimum number of team members that have to disappear before a project stalls; a measure of risk resulting from information being held by too few people.

Example usage: Appears in *Chapter 16 (Pillar 7 – Collaboration and Culture)* (context: myth of the lone genius)

Related pillars: Collaboration | Reliability

Chaos Engineering

The discipline of experimenting on a system in order to build confidence in the system's capability to withstand turbulent conditions in production.

Example usage: Appears in *Chapter 14 (Pillar 5 – Reliability and Resilience)* (context: testing safety nets)

Related pillars: Reliability | Observability

Circuit Breaker

A design pattern that detects failures and encapsulates the logic of preventing a failure from constantly recurring during maintenance, temporary external failure, or unexpected system difficulties.

Example usage: Appears in *Chapter 14 (Pillar 5 – Reliability and Resilience)* (context: preventing cascading failures)

Related pillars: Reliability | Architecture

Clean Architecture

An architectural style where dependencies point inward toward policies, isolating business rules from frameworks and infrastructure (also known as ports and adapters).

Example usage: Appears in *Chapter 13 (Pillar 4 – Architecture and Design)* (context: dependency rule and diagram)

Related pillars: Architecture

Co-Pilot Mindset

An active engagement model where the engineer directs, reviews, and owns the AI's output, rather than passively accepting it as a finished product.

Example usage: Appears in *Chapter 6 (The Human – AI Collaboration)* (context: treating AI as a tireless intern)

Related pillars: Reliability | Security

Code Smell

A surface indication in code (like duplication or long methods) that usually corresponds to a deeper problem in the system's design.

Example usage: Appears in *Chapter 9 (The Discipline of Refactoring)* (context: symptoms of decay)

Related pillars: Architecture | Reliability

Cognitive Load

The amount of mental effort required to understand a piece of code, directly impacted by complexity, naming, and structure.

Example usage: Appears in *Chapter 7 (Code is for Humans First, Computers Second)* (context: short-term memory limits)

Related pillars: Architecture | Reliability

Cohesion

The degree to which elements inside a module belong together; high cohesion ensures that things changing together stay together.

Example usage: Appears in *Chapter 13 (Pillar 4 – Architecture and Design)* (context: utensil tray analogy)

Related pillars: Architecture

Compiler Fallacy

The mistaken belief that if code compiles and runs, the engineering work is complete, ignoring the human cost of maintenance.

Example usage: Appears in *Chapter 7 (Code is for Humans First, Computers Second)* (context: intro hook)

Related pillars: Lifecycle | Reliability

Configuration Drift

The phenomenon where servers in an environment become increasingly different from one another (and from the desired state) due to manual ad-hoc changes.

Example usage: Appears in *Chapter 10 (Pillar 1 – Lifecycle Management)* (context: solved by IaC)

Related pillars: Lifecycle | Reliability

Continuous Delivery (CD)

The practice of automating the release process so that code changes are always in a deployable state.

Example usage: Appears in *Chapter 10 (Pillar 1 – Lifecycle Management)* (context: the conveyor belt to production)

Related pillars: Lifecycle

Continuous Integration (CI)

The practice of merging code changes into a central repository frequently, triggering automated builds and tests to detect errors early.

Example usage: Appears in *Chapter 10 (Pillar 1 – Lifecycle Management)* (context: the gatekeeper of quality)

Related pillars: Lifecycle | Reliability

Contract Test

A test ensuring a service's interface meets explicit consumer expectations (fields, formats, error codes) without invoking full downstream systems.

Example usage: Appears in *Chapter 10 (Pillar 1 – Lifecycle Management)* (context: boundary verification)

Related pillars: Lifecycle | Reliability | Architecture

Correlation ID

A unique identifier attached to a request that propagates across all services, allowing disparate logs and traces to be stitched into a single narrative.

Example usage: Appears in *Chapter 12 (Pillar 3 Observability – Building Systems You Can See and Understand)* (context: middleware example)

Related pillars: Observability | Architecture

Coupling

The degree of interdependence between software modules; high coupling makes systems hard to change because changes ripple through connections.

Example usage: Appears in *Chapter 13 (Pillar 4 – Architecture and Design)* (context: junk drawer analogy)

Related pillars: Architecture | Reliability

Data Catalog

A centralized inventory of data assets that provides metadata (ownership, schema, description) to make data discoverable and understandable for engineers.

Example usage: Appears in *Chapter 15 (Pillar 6 – Data and Knowledge Management)* (context: city map analogy)

Related pillars: Observability | Architecture

Data Contract

An agreement between data producers and consumers defining the schema, semantics, and service levels (SLAs) of the data being exchanged, treating data as a product.

Example usage: Appears in *Chapter 15 (Pillar 6 – Data and Knowledge Management)* (context: library vs hoarder analogy)

Related pillars: Architecture | Reliability

Data Gravity

The concept that as data accumulates, it becomes harder to move and attracts more applications and services, making the underlying architecture difficult to change.

Example usage: Appears in *Chapter 15 (Pillar 6 – Data and Knowledge Management)* (context: introduction to data inertia)

Related pillars: Architecture | Lifecycle

Data Lineage

The visualization of data flow through a system, tracking its origin, transformations, and destination to understand dependencies and impact of changes.

Example usage: Appears in *Chapter 15 (Pillar 6 – Data and Knowledge Management)* (context: city map analogy)

Related pillars: Observability | Architecture

Decomposition

Breaking down complex problems into smaller, well-defined sub-tasks that can be solved independently, then integrated – a critical skill for managing both human and AI collaborators.

Example usage: Appears in *Chapter 2 (From Code to Systems: The Evolution of Engineering Thinking)* (context: key skill for AI-era engineering)

Related pillars: Architecture | Lifecycle

Defense in Depth

A security strategy using multiple independent layers of controls so that if one fails, others remain to protect the system.

Example usage: Appears in *Chapter 11 (Pillar 2: Security)* (context: castle analogy for layered security)

Related pillars: Security | Architecture

Dependency Injection

A design pattern where dependencies are provided to a component rather than hardcoded, promoting loose coupling and testability.

Example usage: Appears in *Chapter 13 (Pillar 4 – Architecture and Design)* (context: Python example)

Related pillars: Architecture | Lifecycle

Distributed Tracing

A method used to profile and monitor applications, especially those built using microservices architecture, by tracking requests as they flow through systems.

Example usage: Appears in *Chapter 12 (Pillar 3 Observability – Building Systems You Can See and Understand)* (context: detective analogy)

Related pillars: Observability | Architecture

DTO (Data Transfer Object)

A simple, neutral data shape used to cross module or service boundaries without exposing internal domain models or persistence types.

Example usage: Appears in *Chapter 13 (Pillar 4 – Architecture and Design)* (context: preventing leaky abstractions)

Related pillars: Architecture

Editor-in-Chief Mindset

The shift in the engineer's role from primarily writing code to reviewing, auditing, and taking responsibility for AI-generated output.

Example usage: Appears in *Chapter 18 (From Tools to Thinking)* (context: newspaper editor analogy)

Related pillars: Reliability | Security

End-to-End (E2E) Test

A test that verifies the system from the user's perspective, exercising the full stack (frontend, backend, database) to ensure critical journeys work.

Example usage: Appears in *Chapter 8 (The Testing Pyramid)* (context: the peak of the pyramid)

Related pillars: Reliability | Lifecycle

Environment Parity

The practice of keeping development, staging, and production environments as similar as possible to prevent "it works on my machine" issues.

Example usage: Appears in *Chapter 10 (Pillar 1 – Lifecycle Management)* (context: reducing deployment risk)

Related pillars: Lifecycle | Reliability

Error Budget

The amount of error that a service can accumulate over a period of time before users are unhappy; the gap between 100% and the SLO.

Example usage: Appears in *Chapter 12 (Pillar 3 Observability – Building Systems You Can See and Understand)* (context: balancing speed and stability)

Related pillars: Observability | Reliability

Feature Flag

A technique to turn functionality on or off during runtime, allowing code to be deployed but not yet active for users.

Example usage: Appears in *Chapter 10 (Pillar 1 – Lifecycle Management)* (context: decoupling deployment from release)

Related pillars: Lifecycle | Reliability

Feedback Loop

A mechanism where a system's outputs inform future inputs, enabling adaptation; in software, realized through monitoring, alerts, and user telemetry.

Example usage: Appears in *Chapter 4 (From Coder to System Thinker)* (context: sequence diagram to staging/monitoring)

Related pillars: Observability | Lifecycle

Fitness Function

An automated, executable check that continuously verifies whether a system or architecture still satisfies a desired quality attribute (e.g., latency, coupling, availability) as it evolves.

Example usage: Appears in *Chapter 13 (Pillar 4 – Architecture and Design)* (context: evolutionary architecture guardrails)

Related pillars: Architecture | Reliability | Observability

Ghost System

A critical system that no current team member understands or knows how to maintain, representing extreme risk and a Bus Factor of zero.

Example usage: Appears in *Chapter 19 (Legacy and Mentorship)* (context: the server under the desk)

Related pillars: Reliability | Collaboration

Guardrail

A lightweight protective mechanism (tests, flags, monitoring) that reduces risk and speeds change by catching issues early.

Example usage: Appears in *Chapter 5 (The Engineering Mindset)* (context: disciplined delivery loop)

Related pillars: Lifecycle | Observability | Reliability

Hallucination

A phenomenon where an AI model generates syntactically correct but factually incorrect or non-existent code, libraries, or facts.

Example usage: Appears in *Chapter 6 (The Human – AI Collaboration)* (context: warning about non-existent libraries)

Related pillars: Reliability | Security

Ice Cream Cone

A testing anti-pattern where a project has many slow E2E tests and few fast unit tests, leading to long feedback loops and high maintenance costs.

Example usage: Appears in *Chapter 8 (The Testing Pyramid)* (context: inverted pyramid consequences)

Related pillars: Lifecycle | Reliability

IDOR (Insecure Direct Object Reference)

An authorization flaw where users can access objects by ID without ownership checks, exposing other tenants' data.

Example usage: Appears in *Chapter 6 (The Human – AI Collaboration)* (context: invoice endpoint ownership)

Related pillars: Security | Reliability

IDOR (Insecure Direct Object References)

A vulnerability where an application exposes direct references to internal objects (like database IDs) without verifying the user's authorization to access them.

Example usage: Appears in *Chapter 11 (Pillar 2: Security)* (context: example of broken access control)

Related pillars: Security

Infrastructure as Code (IaC)

Managing and provisioning computing infrastructure through machine-readable definition files rather than physical hardware configuration or interactive configuration tools.

Example usage: Appears in *Chapter 10 (Pillar 1 – Lifecycle Management)* (context: treating servers like software)

Related pillars: Lifecycle | Architecture

Integration Test

A test that verifies the interaction between two or more components (e.g., service and database) to ensure they collaborate correctly across boundaries.

Example usage: Appears in *Chapter 8 (The Testing Pyramid)* (context: the middle layer)

Related pillars: Architecture | Reliability

Irreversible Decision

A choice whose reversal is expensive or disruptive ("one-way door"), requiring deeper upfront evaluation and broader stakeholder input.

Example usage: Appears in *Chapter 5 (The Engineering Mindset)* (context: database selection)

Related pillars: Architecture | Reliability

Knowledge Silo

A situation where critical knowledge is held by one person or a small group and not shared, creating bottlenecks and risk for the organization.

Example usage: Appears in *Chapter 16 (Pillar 7 – Collaboration and Culture)* (context: target audience connection)

Related pillars: Collaboration

Last Responsible Moment

The latest point a decision can be made before delay costs exceed commitment costs, allowing better information gathering without incurring risk from indecision.

Example usage: Appears in *Chapter 13 (Pillar 4 – Architecture and Design)* (context: one-way vs two-way doors)

Related pillars: Architecture | Lifecycle

Legacy Code

Code that has been successful enough to survive; often used pejoratively, but represents value delivered. The goal is to make it maintainable.

Example usage: Appears in *Chapter 19 (Legacy and Mentorship)* (context: reframing legacy as success)

Related pillars: Lifecycle | Architecture

Lifecycle Management (ALM)

The continuous process of managing a software application from initial planning and coding through testing, deployment, and eventual retirement.

Example usage: Appears in *Chapter 10 (Pillar 1 – Lifecycle Management)* (context: the factory floor of software)

Related pillars: Lifecycle

Local Optimization

An improvement that benefits a single component while degrading overall system behavior, typically by violating contracts, invariants, or downstream assumptions.

Example usage: Appears in *Chapter 4 (From Coder to System Thinker)* (context: tunnel vision harms the whole)

Related pillars: Architecture | Reliability

Mental Model

An internal representation of how a system works, enabling engineers to predict behavior, identify problems, and make architectural decisions without needing to inspect every detail.

Example usage: Appears in *Chapter 2 (From Code to Systems: The Evolution of Engineering Thinking)* (context: why experienced engineers adapt to AI tools easily)

Related pillars: Architecture | Observability

Mentorship

An engineering discipline focused on transferring knowledge and capability to others, scaling impact and reducing the Bus Factor.

Example usage: Appears in *Chapter 19 (Legacy and Mentorship)* (context: seniority measured by enablement)

Related pillars: Collaboration

Novelty Tax

Extra cost (time, instability, cognitive load) paid when adopting unfamiliar technology before its benefits justify disruption.

Example usage: Appears in *Chapter 5 (The Engineering Mindset)* (context: evaluating "boring" tech value)

Related pillars: Architecture | Reliability | Lifecycle

Observability

The property of a system that allows understanding its internal state purely by inspecting its external outputs (logs, metrics, traces).

Example usage: Appears in *Chapter 12 (Pillar 3 Observability – Building Systems You Can See and Understand)* (context: difference between guessing and knowing)

Related pillars: Observability | Reliability

One-Way Door

A decision that is difficult or expensive to reverse (e.g., database choice), requiring careful deliberation and data gathering.

Example usage: Appears in *Chapter 13 (Pillar 4 – Architecture and Design)* (context: Amazon decision model)

Related pillars: Architecture | Lifecycle

Principle of Least Astonishment

Code should behave in a way that minimizes confusion for the reader; the implementation should match the intent implied by the interface.

Example usage: Appears in *Chapter 7 (Code is for Humans First, Computers Second)* (context: intent vs implementation)

Related pillars: Architecture | Reliability

Principle of Least Privilege

The practice of granting only the minimum permissions necessary for a user or service to perform its function, limiting potential damage.

Example usage: Appears in *Chapter 11 (Pillar 2: Security)* (context: hotel key card analogy)

Related pillars: Security

Problem Framing

The engineering skill of defining constraints, inputs, and edge cases so precisely that an AI or system can generate a correct solution; the new "syntax" of engineering.

Example usage: Appears in *Chapter 18 (From Tools to Thinking)* (context: genie in a lamp analogy)

Related pillars: Architecture | Lifecycle

Progressive Delivery

A release strategy that separates deployment from release, allowing features to be rolled out gradually to a subset of users to limit risk.

Example usage: Appears in *Chapter 10 (Pillar 1 – Lifecycle Management)* (context: controlling the blast radius)

Related pillars: Lifecycle | Reliability

Prompt Engineering

The practice of crafting precise inputs to guide AI models toward specific, high-quality technical outputs, effectively acting as a technical specification.

Example usage: Appears in *Chapter 6 (The Human – AI Collaboration)* (context: rubber duck debugging on steroids)

Related pillars: Lifecycle | Architecture

Psychological Safety

A shared belief that the team is safe for interpersonal risk-taking, allowing members to speak up with ideas, questions, concerns, or mistakes without fear of punishment.

Example usage: Appears in *Chapter 16 (Pillar 7 – Collaboration and Culture)* (context: foundation of engineering culture)

Related pillars: Collaboration

Refactoring

The process of changing a software system in such a way that it does not alter the external behavior of the code yet improves its internal structure.

Example usage: Appears in *Chapter 9 (The Discipline of Refactoring)* (context: core chapter concept)

Related pillars: Architecture | Lifecycle

Reliability

The probability that a system will perform its intended function without failure for a specific period under stated conditions; doing what you promised to do.

Example usage: Appears in *Chapter 14 (Pillar 5 – Reliability and Resilience)* (context: core definition vs resilience)

Related pillars: Reliability | Lifecycle

Resilience

The ability of a system to recover quickly from difficulties, adapt to changing conditions, and degrade gracefully rather than collapsing under stress.

Example usage: Appears in *Chapter 14 (Pillar 5 – Reliability and Resilience)* (context: core definition vs reliability)

Related pillars: Reliability | Architecture

Reversible Decision

A choice that can be changed with low cost and limited ripple effects ("two-way door"), enabling experimentation without heavy long-term commitment.

Example usage: Appears in *Chapter 5 (The Engineering Mindset)* (context: interface seam for storage)

Related pillars: Architecture | Lifecycle

Ripple Effect

The propagation of a change in one component through dependent components, often amplifying impact when contracts are implicit or untested.

Example usage: Appears in *Chapter 4 (From Coder to System Thinker)* (context: diagram of change propagation)

Related pillars: Architecture | Reliability

Rollback Strategy

A pre-planned procedure to revert a failed deployment to the last known good state, typically using the Detect-Decide-Revert loop.

Example usage: Appears in *Chapter 10 (Pillar 1 – Lifecycle Management)* (context: hope is not a strategy)

Related pillars: Lifecycle | Reliability

Row-Level Authorization

Enforcing access at the individual record level so only owners (or permitted roles) can read or modify specific rows.

Example usage: Appears in *Chapter 6 (The Human – AI Collaboration)* (context: per-tenant invoice access)

Related pillars: Security | Architecture

Schema Evolution

The practice of changing a database schema over time without downtime, often using patterns like “Expand and Contract” to maintain compatibility.

Example usage: Appears in *Chapter 15 (Pillar 6 – Data and Knowledge Management)* (context: renovating a train station)

Related pillars: Lifecycle | Architecture

Secure by Design

An approach where security is a core requirement from the initial architecture phase, ensuring default configurations are safe.

Example usage: Appears in *Chapter 11 (Pillar 2: Security)* (context: car safety features analogy)

Related pillars: Security | Architecture

Semantic Versioning (SemVer)

A versioning standard (Major.Minor.Patch) that conveys meaning about the underlying changes and compatibility of a software release.

Example usage: Appears in *Chapter 10 (Pillar 1 – Lifecycle Management)* (context: contract of compatibility)

Related pillars: Lifecycle | Reliability

Single Responsibility Principle (SRP)

A function or module should have one, and only one, reason to change.

Example usage: Appears in *Chapter 7 (Code is for Humans First, Computers Second)* (context: encapsulating complexity)

Related pillars: Architecture | Lifecycle

SLI (Service Level Indicator)

A quantitative measure of some aspect of the level of service that is provided, such as latency or error rate.

Example usage: Appears in *Chapter 12 (Pillar 3 Observability – Building Systems You Can See and Understand)* (context: defining "healthy")

Related pillars: Observability | Reliability

SLO (Service Level Objective)

A target value or range of values for a service level that is measured by an SLI.

Example usage: Appears in *Chapter 12 (Pillar 3 Observability – Building Systems You Can See and Understand)* (context: defining targets vs promises); also in *Chapter 14 (Pillar 5 – Reliability and Resilience)* (context: cost of nines and error budgets).

Related pillars: Observability | Reliability

Software Entropy

The tendency for software to become difficult and expensive to maintain as it evolves, leading to "rot" or a "Big Ball of Mud" if not actively managed.

Example usage: Appears in *Chapter 9 (The Discipline of Refactoring)* (context: introduction to decay)

Related pillars: Architecture | Lifecycle

Stewardship

The mindset of caring for code and systems for the benefit of the team and future maintainers, rather than asserting personal ownership or territory.

Example usage: Appears in *Chapter 16 (Pillar 7 – Collaboration and Culture)* (context: ownership vs stewardship)

Related pillars: Collaboration | Lifecycle

Structured Logging

Recording log events as machine-readable objects (e.g., JSON) rather than plain text, enabling aggregation, filtering, and analysis.

Example usage: Appears in *Chapter 12 (Pillar 3 Observability – Building Systems You Can See and Understand)* (context: TypeScript example of JSON logs)

Related pillars: Observability

Syntax Generation

The mechanical act of producing code syntax, which is becoming a commodity performed by AI, shifting human value toward design and verification.

Example usage: Appears in *Chapter 18 (From Tools to Thinking)* (context: comparison to manual arithmetic)

Related pillars: Lifecycle

Systems Thinking

Reasoning about software as interconnected components with responsibilities, interactions, and trade-offs, rather than isolated functions – the foundation of scalable, maintainable architecture.

Example usage: Appears in *Chapter 2 (From Code to Systems: The Evolution of Engineering Thinking)* (context: essential skill for AI-era engineering)

Related pillars: Architecture | Reliability | Observability

Technical Debt

The implied cost of additional rework caused by choosing an easy (limited) solution now instead of using a better approach that would take longer.

Example usage: Appears in *Chapter 9 (The Discipline of Refactoring)* (context: Boy Scout Rule)

Related pillars: Architecture | Lifecycle

Technical Debt Interest

Recurring extra effort caused by a shortcut, expressed as time per change multiplied by change frequency.

Example usage: Appears in *Chapter 5 (The Engineering Mindset)* (context: debt register ranking)

Related pillars: Lifecycle | Architecture | Reliability

Testing Pyramid

A strategy for structuring tests to optimize feedback speed and cost, emphasizing many fast unit tests, fewer integration tests, and very few slow E2E tests.

Example usage: Appears in *Chapter 8 (The Testing Pyramid)* (context: core chapter concept)

Related pillars: Lifecycle | Reliability

Threat Modeling

A structured process of identifying potential security threats and vulnerabilities during the design phase to plan effective mitigations.

Example usage: Appears in *Chapter 11 (Pillar 2: Security)* (context: four key questions for design)

Related pillars: Security | Architecture

Two-Way Door

A decision that is easily reversible (e.g., variable name) and should be made quickly to maintain velocity.

Example usage: Appears in *Chapter 13 (Pillar 4 – Architecture and Design)* (context: Amazon decision model)

Related pillars: Architecture | Lifecycle

Ubiquitous Language

A shared vocabulary between developers and domain experts used in both conversation and code to prevent translation errors.

Example usage: Appears in *Chapter 13 (Pillar 4 – Architecture and Design)* (context: Domain-Driven Design)

Related pillars: Architecture | Collaboration

Unit Test

A fast, isolated test that verifies the logic of a single component (function or class) without external dependencies like databases or networks.

Example usage: Appears in *Chapter 8 (The Testing Pyramid)* (context: the base of the pyramid)

Related pillars: Lifecycle | Architecture

Zero Trust

A security model that assumes no user or system is trustworthy by default, requiring verification for every request regardless of origin.

Example usage: Appears in *Chapter 11 (Pillar 2: Security)* (context: core mindset of modern security)

Related pillars: Security

Chapter 22:

Author's Biography

build smart. design better. architect future.
— Dmytro Golodiuk

The trajectory of software engineering in the early 21st century is defined by a shift from isolated, monolithic systems to interconnected, intelligent ecosystems. The career of Dmytro Golodiuk serves as a case study of this evolution. Spanning more than seventeen years, his professional narrative is not merely a list of roles; it is a map of the industry's transformation from on-premise application development to distributed, cloud-native, and AI-augmented enterprise architectures. From his early days deeply embedded in the Microsoft .NET ecosystem to his current standing in Enterprise Agentic AI and regu-

latory technology (RegTech), Dmytro embodies the archetype of the "Business-First Architect".

His professional life is characterized by a dual competency: deep technical mastery of the Microsoft stack (Azure, Dynamics 365, .NET) and a sophisticated grasp of enterprise strategy (TOGAF, ArchiMate, DORA compliance). This combination allows him to operate at the intersection of board-level strategy and high-performance engineering. Whether establishing the Enterprise Architecture function for a multinational holding like the Zeppelin Group or designing mission-critical regulatory systems for the Central Bank of Ireland, his work consistently demonstrates that technology is a lever for business resilience and growth, rather than an end in itself.

This biography traces Dmytro Golodiuk's journey through the lens of architectural evolution. It explores his academic foundations, his formative years in software development, his decade of transformation at Zeppelin Group, his specialized consultancy in the high-stakes financial sector, and his voice for the future of AI engineering through his "ArchiCraft"[1] platform. Together, these stages reveal an architect who treats software not just as code, but as a living, strategic asset.

Academic origins and the cybernetic mindset

The intellectual foundation of Dmytro Golodiuk's career was laid in the rigorous academic environment of Ukraine, a region recognized

[1] ArchiCraft is Dmytro Golodiuk's presence in the virtual world via a personal blog, podcast, and LinkedIn Newsletter about Enterprise Architecture, Solution Architecture, Engineering Management, and AI.

for producing engineering talent with strong mathematical and theoretical underpinnings. His journey began at Lutsk Gymnasium #21, where his curriculum focused on Physics, Math, Biology, and Chemistry. This early immersion in the hard sciences instilled a disciplined, analytical approach to problem-solving that would later define his architectural style, which prioritizes empirical evidence and structural integrity over fleeting trends.

His formal higher education commenced at Lesya Ukrainka Volyn National University, where he earned a Master's degree in Computer Science (2004–2010). During this period, his potential became evident to peers and mentors alike. He was a finalist in the "Student of The Year" competitions for the "Computer Genius" nomination in consecutive years (2008 and 2009) and was recognized as the "Best Young Programmer". These accolades were more than academic honors; they signaled an early aptitude for algorithmic thinking and the practical application of computer science principles.

He did not stop at a generalist computer science education. Dmytro pursued postgraduate studies in Cybernetics at Taras Shevchenko National University of Kyiv (2010–2013). Cybernetics, the scientific study of control and communication in complex systems, provides a unique and powerful lens for a future enterprise architect. Where traditional computer science often focuses on the efficiency of individual algorithms, cybernetics emphasizes systems thinking, feedback loops, and the behavior of complex systems under change. This academic backdrop is visible in his later architectural philosophies, especially his focus on the "Sense-Plan-Act" cycle in AI agents and his holistic view of enterprise systems as living organisms rather than static structures.

From .NET engineer to enterprise architect

The early phase of Dmytro's professional journey was rooted in the Microsoft .NET ecosystem. Working close to the code, he built and maintained applications on top of the Microsoft stack, gaining practical experience with real-world constraints, performance considerations, and integration challenges. This period grounded him in the realities of software delivery: deadlines, trade-offs, and the constant negotiation between elegance and practicality.

Over time, his focus expanded from individual applications to the systems that connected them. The same cybernetic mindset that shaped his academic work now guided his professional evolution. Rather than treating each project as an isolated effort, he began to see patterns of control, feedback, and coordination across entire organizations. This systems view naturally pulled him toward architecture: defining boundaries, contracts, and flows so that many teams could move quickly without losing coherence.

Zeppelin Group: building enterprise architecture function

That shift from project-level delivery to organizational design crystallized during his work with the Zeppelin Group, a multinational holding. There, Dmytro played a central role in establishing the Enterprise Architecture function. Instead of focusing purely on technology choices, he worked at the junction of strategy and implementation: translating board-level ambitions into concrete architectural principles, reference models, and roadmaps.

This was not architecture as documentation, but architecture as a continuous practice. In a group setting with many business units, platforms, and legacy systems, he helped define how the organization would modernize: moving from on-premise solutions to distributed, cloud-native architectures while keeping critical operations stable. The work demanded both technical depth and the ability to speak the language of executives, linking design decisions to resilience, risk reduction, and long-term competitiveness.

RegTech and mission-critical financial systems

After his pivotal decade of transformation at Zeppelin Group, Dmytro applied his experience in an even more regulated and high-stakes context: the financial sector. Designing mission-critical regulatory systems for the Central Bank of Ireland required a synthesis of his core strengths: precise engineering, systems thinking, and a strong sense of accountability.

Regulatory technology (RegTech) operates under constraints where failure is not merely inconvenient; it can carry systemic consequences. In this environment, architectures must support auditability, transparency, and predictable behavior under stress. Dmytro's background in cybernetics and enterprise architecture equipped him to design systems that could both enforce rules and adapt to evolving regulatory expectations, helping institutions respond to change without sacrificing control.

Enterprise Agentic AI and the ArchiCraft platform

As AI systems matured from tools to semi-autonomous agents, Dmytro focused his attention on Enterprise Agentic AI: how intelligent agents can be embedded into serious, regulated environments without compromising safety or trust. His cybernetic roots again proved relevant. The same principles of sense, plan, and act that describe biological and mechanical systems became a framework for thinking about AI assistants interacting with complex enterprises.

Through his "ArchiCraft" platform, he began to articulate this perspective more publicly. ArchiCraft presents architecture as a craft discipline: grounded in principles, informed by practice, and responsible to the organizations it serves. In the context of AI, that means designing agentic systems that are observable, controllable, and aligned with business intent rather than deployed as opaque black boxes.

The "Business-First Architect"

Across these domains, a consistent theme emerges: Dmytro sees technology as a means, not an end. The label "Business-First Architect" captures this stance. It does not imply an absence of technical depth; instead, it insists that technical decisions must be justified in terms of business outcomes, resilience, and strategic positioning.

His dual competency in the Microsoft stack and enterprise strategy frameworks such as TOGAF, ArchiMate, and DORA compliance allows him to mediate between worlds that often misunderstand each other. To executives, he translates architectural diagrams into narratives about risk, adaptability, and opportunity. To engineers, he translates strategic goals into concrete design choices, guiding them toward systems that can evolve without collapsing under their own complexity.

Mentorship and legacy

Behind the titles, there is a consistent thread of mentorship. The curiosity that drove him from gymnasium science courses to cybernetics research now shapes how he works with the next generation. By sharing methodologies and talks under the ArchiCraft umbrella, he encourages aspiring architects to see beyond individual tools and frameworks.

Dmytro Golodiuk emerges not just as a specialist in Microsoft technologies, enterprise architecture, or RegTech, but as a practitioner of thoughtful engineering. His journey models the mindset this book advocates: systems-oriented, principled, and anchored in the belief that well-designed software is a strategic asset that can carry organizations through technological change.

Staying up to date

If this book resonates with you, I would love to stay connected. I share ideas in the same spirit as these chapters: practical, principle-first, and shaped by what works in real systems.

Book website (updates and resources): https://foundations.golodiuk.com

Personal website (writing and background): https://www.golodiuk.com

Blog "ArchiCraft News": https://www.golodiuk.com/news

LinkedIn (notes and professional updates): https://www.linkedin.com/in/dimanngo/

Podcast "ArchiCraft: Solution Architecture Insights for AI Engineering": https://pod.link/1822823301

If you would like more direct guidance, you can also find my **mentor** profile here (session options and booking): https://mentor.sh/mentors/dmytro_golodiuk

Index

www.ingramcontent.com/pod-product-compliance
Lightning Source LLC
LaVergne TN
LVHW052248200926
848481LV00002B/309
* 9 7 9 8 2 3 3 0 5 1 0 3 6 *